Praise for Ruby's Trust

Jesus looked people in the eyes when He talked to them, disarming self-consciousness and fear. In His presence they felt an absence of shame and the desire to be themselves more fully. Cy DeBoer does the same. Whether decked to the nines at an inaugural ball or behind the barbed wire fence of a prison, Cy looks people square in the eyes. It was a privilege to have a front row seat to the early days of Ruby and Cy's friendship. Moving overseas in 2001, I loved hearing updates of their tales of adventure, heartache, and deep friendship. Back on furlough, I stood at the curb of the house on the road named Ruby Trust, marveling at God's intimate care of Ruby and Cy. This is a gospel story of a true friendship that has inspired me to look people in the eyes and expect God to do something wonderful.

Kourtney Street
Vice President
Internal Communication and Culture, FamilyLife

In Ruby's Trust, Cy DeBoer beautifully tells the much-needed story of unconditional love and friendship. *Ruby's Trust* takes you on a thoughtful journey, exploring a world that most don't know or think about. DeBoer quickly has you thinking deeply about the unknown stories that every person has and that so many hide. DeBoer weaves humor throughout as she reveals the heartbreaking reality of people alone in the world, who are often judged or treated as invisible.

On every page you absorb subtle and important insight for how to give genuine care and be mindful of your motives. You can't read this book without reflecting on your own life and relationships. This beautiful story leaves you wondering what you might be missing as you go through your life, and how you can keep your eyes and heart open to see them. *Ruby's Trust* is honest, inspiring, and thought provoking. It's one of those books that stays with you long after reading it, because Ruby makes her way into your heart, and she stays there.

Paula DuPre' Pesmen
Nonprofit Executive Director
Grammy Award–winning film producer

Ruby's Trust is a beautiful reminder of sacrificial love that was not only shown to Ruby and her brother, but that we as Christians should live out on a daily basis! I picture Jesus beaming with such joy as God willing millions will read this book and follow the steps modeled to love as Christ loves us. God wrote a beautiful story through Cy and His words.

Brett Garretson
Pastoral Care Director
Cherry Hills Community Church

What if? In this endearing and unforgettable journey, author Cy DeBoer gives us the answer. What if we took the time and gave the compassion to someone truly in need? What if we set aside our personal needs and truly gave of ourselves to someone who could never repay us? And what if the stranger we befriended, fed, clothed, and welcomed under our roof—the least of these—truly was Jesus? *Ruby's Trust* focuses on one author, one homeless woman, and one shared journey, and in so doing reveals much about all of us — and about those strangers we too often walk by without so much as a smile.

Jimmy Patterson
Author of *A History of Character:*
The Story of Midland, Texas

Ruby's Trust is a story that has to be told. DeBoer tells a true story that affects all of us, if we allow it. Cy weaves truth, humor, faith, honor, and humility into a fabric so loving and beautiful that it patches our ragged society and gives us all hope. Couldn't put it down.

Rhonda Vickers
Writer, Artist

I'm sitting here with tears streaming down my face and with joy in my heart. I have just finished reading *Ruby's Trust* and my heart is filled with so many emotions. But the biggest one is how precious and amazing is God's love for *all* of us!

Ruby's Trust so accurately captures our fears, uncertainty, and doubt when faced with circumstances we are convinced we aren't equipped to meet. While simultaneously making it clear that God is present in everything and that with trust, faith, obedience, and great sense of humor, we, as followers of Christ, are able to make a difference in the world around us. Cy DeBoer has captured her journey with Ruby with honesty, tenderness, thoughtfulness, and her wonderful sense of humor. A delightful, awe-inspiring read.

Leslie Franz
The Girlz Bible Study

Ruby's Trust was an amazing journey where two unlikely people not only became friends, they actually ended up "saving" one another. *Ruby's Trust* truly put a face on homelessness for me. Ruby's struggles as well as her wonderful unique personality jumped off the pages. Cy DeBoer's ability to write with humor made both her and Ruby endearing. There were also plenty of touching moments. I personally loved how spiritual truth and mystery were woven in throughout the pages.

I highly recommend *Ruby's Trust* to anyone wanting a funny, serendipitous read. Expect to fall in love with Cy and Ruby and be challenged to engage people outside of your normal circles.

Lara Press
Therapist

This is a beautifully written story of Jesus at work. From "Jesus Shoved Me" you will see the trials, tears, and joys of a very unlikely friendship. The author's humor, candor, and honesty will warm hearts and encourage the reader to learn what can happen when two very different worlds collide. With Cy's ears and heart focused on Jesus, miracles and trust become an unlikely but incredible reality. I couldn't put it down. Belly laughs and a trail of tears put me on roller coaster of emotions propelled by love.

Martha Parsley
Human Resources

This is a story from the heart about faith transcending economic boundaries and stereotypes. Seldom do we take the opportunity that Cy took, to learn from people who, on the surface, are very different from who we are and who we expect them to be. Ruby and Cy's relationship inspires us to risk our hearts and be open to possibilities we may not fully understand.

Leslie R. Foster
President & CEO
The Gathering Place

An inspiring true story of how the author and Ruby learned to move beyond their personal discomforts in a most unexpected relationship that begins with the intersection of two women's lives who are traveling vastly different roads in the world. Author Cy DeBoer's deeply intimate relationship with Jesus gives her the courage to act on behalf of Ruby, resulting in a beautiful unfolding of both women receiving the gift of unwavering trust in Christ and one another.

Erin Nevers
Health Care Advocate

I am forever changed by this true story of a lady sitting on a curb by a busy street and the curious, caring lady she meets. Go on this journey with them and you will not forget it! This engaging read is well told, compassionate, and witty. Pulling on your heartstrings it will make you smile, laugh, and cry. God has a plan for all of us if we search our hearts and act when He nudges us to open that door and step out in faith as Cy DeBoer did!

Cheri Issel
Advocate for homeless women

When Cy DeBoer gives a homeless woman a ride, that single good deed takes on a life of its own—and what ensues is both hilarious and poignant. *Ruby's Trust* tells the story of an unlikely friendship and a remarkable journey. I can't recommend this book enough! I promise you'll laugh. You'll cry. You might even find yourself inspired to find your own Ruby on the side of the road.

Karen Linamen Bouchard
Author
Just Hand Over the Chocolate and No One Will Get Hurt

Cy DeBoer has written a compelling book that captivates and inspires. Her true story told with humor and compassion is about two incomparable women whose lives intersect in a rare moment of faith. It reinforces for us all the power of acceptance, forgiveness, and love resulting in *Ruby's Trust*.

Judy Weaver
Retired Medical Professional

RUBY'S TRUST

CY DEBOER

Illumify Media Global · Littleton, Colorado

The views and opinions expressed in this book are those of the author and do
not necessarily reflect the official policy or position of Illumify Media Global.

Unless otherwise noted, all Scripture is from the Holy Bible New International
Version®, NIV® Copyright ©1973, 1978, 1984, 2011 by Biblica, Inc.® Used by
permission. All rights reserved worldwide.

Published by
Illumify Media Global
www.IllumifyMedia.com
"Write. Market. Publish. SELL!"

A portion of the proceeds from Ruby's Trust will be donated to:
There with Care (therewithcare.org), The Gathering Place (tgpdenver.org), and
Manna Ministries, Inc. (www.Mannaministry.net).

Library of Congress Control Number: 2019907734

Paperback ISBN: 978-1-949021-37-0
eBook ISBN: 978-1-949021-38-7

Typeset by Art Innovations (http://artinnovations.in/)
Cover design by Debbie Lewis

Printed in the United States of America

My prayer is this story will honor the memory of my mother Jo Gulick, who taught me the true meaning of mercy and imparted my desire to share it.

Ruby's Trust is dedicated with love to my husband, Bruce, a man of faith who is loving, kind, merciful, wise, and infinitely patient. He put me on a pedestal thirty-six years ago and catches me when I fall off—every single day.

Contents

Foreword

Why Reading Ruby's Trust is a Gift to Give Yourself

Cy and I have known each other since we were thirteen, but as adults we've lived in different parts of the country. Though we've stayed in touch all these years, living in different cities has meant that we've had to share our lives in shorthand rather than in full-blown detail.

Over time, I heard about Ruby in bits and pieces, but bits and pieces do not do the story justice.

From the minute you open the book, you know you are going to have an interesting ride. The story moves quickly—and with self-deprecating humor—to tell how Cy leaves her Bible Study group and stops to check on a homeless woman and her dog outside the church.

Over time, Cy and her husband Bruce, an attorney, find themselves stepping in to help Ruby navigate life. They see the challenges of the welfare system through Ruby's eyes. Cy and Ruby encounter obstacles, but they also find kindness from others.

Though Cy's actions are often saintly, throughout the book,

she lets us see that she is human. Cy admits there were days when she thought of pulling the covers over her head instead of getting involved in another Ruby adventure.

Despite these occasional leanings, Cy somehow finds her inner angel.

With this very beautiful and humorous story, Cy paints a picture of those who are less fortunate. They are not there because they aren't trying. They are there because the obstacles in their path are often too daunting to face alone.

Ruby's Trust uplifts and expands our hearts. With her testimony and this book, Cy makes us all better people.

Kate Kelly, Author, Historian
America Comes Alive

Acknowledgments

Who has a husband that is willing to let a stranger his wife found on a curb spend the night in the bedroom down the hall from him? I do! Thank you, Bruce DeBoer for never discouraging me from finding ways we can help others. You have walked in faith with me and because of your love, kindness and generosity, I was able to write this book.

Thank you to our children, Ryan and Whitney, for your warm and willing acceptance of Ruby into our family. Thank you for encouraging me to write in the first place by laughing at my annual Groundhog's Day letters.

Thank you to my mother, who kept a pen and paper near her at all times and showed me how cathartic writing can be. Also, thank you for correcting errors in my letters with a red pen, then promptly returning them edited.

Bible Studies are more than studying the Bible. I want to thank The Girlz, my Tuesday morning group of the dearest women and prayer warriors a girl could ever hope share life with every week. Thank you for your diligent prayers for Ruby and her brother.

Thank you to the Gathering Place, the women and children's shelter where I first held a homeless child in my arms and my heart was changed forever.

Thank you to Michael Klassen and Illumify Media Group for believing this story could actually be a book. A huge hug and thank you to Karen Bouchard, my book coach, who got my sense humor and poured her wit and wisdom into keeping me on track as I churned out chapters. Thank you also, to Geoff Stone for his editing expertise. Thank you to Debbie Lewis for the perfect cover depicting the beautiful ruby gem I picked up near a rough asphalt road. Great job!

To Miss Tookey, my high school English teacher, thank you. I guess I was paying more attention than either of us thought.

Thanks to all my friends and family who were always saying "You should write a book." Here you go!

Most importantly, thank you to Jesus for trusting our family with the lives of Ruby and Sam and guiding us so faithfully through uncharted territory.

Thank you, dearest Ruby for your trust.

I am only one,
But still I am one.
I cannot do everything,
But still I can do something;
And because I cannot do everything,
I will not refuse to do
Something that I can do.

Edward Everett Hale

ONE

Jesus Shoved Me, This I Know

---

*G*radually, the well-meaning ladies backed their way out of the circle until I was the last woman standing. It wasn't that the others didn't *want* to help; it's that they had been told in no uncertain terms that their assistance wasn't needed.

In fact, the exact words they'd heard were, "Leave me be; go on about your own business," the woman on the ground growled repeatedly. Eventually they'd thought it best to respect her wishes and had backed away.

I was about to do the same, but instead of backing away I moved in closer.

Before I knew it, I was on my knees, on a worn-out blanket by the curb of a busy street with a scowling woman on one side and a snarling terrier on the other side of me.

What had brought me there? There was only one logical explanation: Jesus shoved me! As I discovered, he is not always wearing his lamb suit when he wants to get your attention.

. . .

THE WHOLE THING had started earlier that morning during a small group Bible study I was leading at a church.

Gwen, one of our group members, had come into the classroom and asked for our attention (not an easy thing to get from a dozen chatty, caffeinated women).

Once we were paying attention, Gwen had explained she'd met a woman she thought was probably homeless, washing her hands and face in the sink next to her in the church restroom.

"I got a little way down the hall before I realized I should have asked how I could help her. I went back to look for her, but she was gone," Gwen told us, clearly unhappy she had missed the chance to help the stranger.

As the small group leader, I'd suggested we pray for the apparently homeless woman right then.

"Dear Lord," I'd prayed, "thank you for giving us the opportunity to pray for this woman who is so heavy on Gwen's heart. Please bring someone You trust to come alongside her wherever she might be. Let her feel Your presence in her life today. Let her know she is loved. Keep her safe, amen."

Leaving the church a couple hours later, I was speed-walking to my car, trying to escape the biting wind. It was an unseasonably chilly day in April and, thanks to the weather man, I had dressed for spring.

I clicked my key fob, opened my car door, and tossed my Bible and notebook in the back seat.

That's when I recognized the concerned ladies from the Wednesday morning Bible study I just attended. They seemed to be gathered in a circle by the curb learning over someone sitting on the ground.

I made a life-changing decision to weather the weather and investigate.

The biting wind whipped against my bare legs as I walked

across the parking lot toward the circle of ladies. I drew closer, I was fairly certain they were standing around the woman we had prayed for earlier that morning. Spread out on the grass was a matted, fuzzy blanket with a faded coyote howling at the moon motif. A woman with long gray-streaked braids twining down the sides of her weathered face sat on the edge of the blanket, leaning her back against a tall pine tree. Her giant glasses were taped together in several places. She was wearing a tattered sweatshirt and pants, one shoe, one slipper, and weariness.

"You hush up Lizzie Lou!" she kept yelling at the dog.

Lizzie Lou was a scruffy little terrier (whitish, grayish, brownish) suffering from a severe identify crisis. She was behaving very Rottweiler-ish. She had the bark and growl down but, seriously, she weighed ten pounds at most. Lizzie Lou was in hyper-protection mode with all of us strangers hovering around her favorite person.

One by one the rest of the ladies reluctantly stepped away from the circle. Next thing I knew, I was alone kneeling in front of the woman on her tattered blanket. I remembered my prayer, asking God to bring someone to come alongside the woman in need. It appeared the someone Jesus had in mind was me.

"Um, hello," I said. "My name is Cy."

Long pause.

I tried again.

"Cy DeBoer. I was just with those women from the church," I added, thinking this woman might like more of an explanation as to why I was kneeling on her blanket. *Heck, I'd like to have a little more explanation myself.*

"I'm Ruby Jean," she said, addressing me for the first time. "And this here is Lizzie Lou."

Lizzie Lou introduced herself with a long growl.

"Can I help you with anything?" I asked.

"Nah."

"Are you hungry? Have you had lunch?" I asked. (Food is always my go-to solution when I don't know what else to offer. My daughter accuses me of having food Tourette's.)

She said she hadn't eaten but was just fine. She explained that the trucker who had dropped her off had given her a granola bar and one of the church ladies had given her a banana.

"Do you need a ride someplace?" I asked, assuming she'd say nah. After all, she looked like she wanted me off her blanket and on my way.

"Nah, I'm thumbing my way to see my brother in Buena Vista."

Oh, thank goodness, she has a brother. That's a relief, I thought. But Buena Vista was a hundred miles away. Hitch-hiking that far to get to a relative didn't sound like a great idea.

"Have you checked on taking the bus? That would be safer." I suggested.

"They don't allow nothin' but a service dog to ride the bus. Ain't like I got the money for no bus anyway." Ruby said, stating the obvious.

"Well, does your brother drive? Can he come get you?"

"He's in prison up there." She replied matter-of-factly.

There went my sense of relief. I gave myself a pep talk. *Okay, Cy don't show any shock. Act like you know lots of people in prison.*

"Oh, well then I guess he won't be driving." I said awkwardly. Lizzie Lou and Ruby's blank stare confirmed my own low opinion of myself at that moment.

Seriously, God, I thought, *you know me. I want to fix this. My heart is aching for this poor woman, but what can I possibly do for her? It doesn't seem like she even wants my help. I should probably just do as she asked and let her be. I don't think I'm prepared for this.*

Prepared? I seemed to hear God ask. *Haven't you been volunteering with homeless women and children for over ten years?*

Well yes, I admitted to Him. *You know I volunteer at the Gathering Place. But most of my time has been spent raising funds for the shelter, serving a few meals, reading to children, speaking to groups.*

Sounds like a good start, God seemed to say. *Now it is time to stop dipping your toes in the water and dive in and get wet! The time has come for you to enlarge your territory.*

Okay Lord, I answered reluctantly, *if You can get her into my car, I'll drive her to the Gathering Place where she can have lunch. Then I'll figure out a way to get her to the mountains to visit her brother.*

Enlarge my territory? The idea was a familiar one, and for good reason! I'd been reading *The Prayer of Jabez,* and for several weeks I'd been praying the very words of Jabez:

Oh, that you would bless me and enlarge my territory! Let your hand be with me, and keep me from harm so that I will be free from pain." And God granted his request. (1 Chronicles 4:10)

Feeling braver, I told Ruby my idea of getting in my car and driving to a woman's shelter. She was not impressed. Apparently, she didn't want to *enlarge her territory.* She just wanted to get to Buena Vista.

"It took me almost two days and twenty bucks to get to this road," she huffed. The road she was near connected with the highway up to the mountains, and she wasn't about to leave that prime location for thumbing a ride. She obviously didn't care for my plan and just wanted me to go away. Lizzie Lou offered her opinion with a low, menacing growl.

"Ruby, I promise I will bring you back to this spot after you have a good lunch and spend a little time warming up out of this cold, crazy wind. I'm freezing! Come on, let's get in my car. Please?" My teeth were chattering.

After more thinking on her part and more shivering on mine, she relented. "You promise, you'll bring me back here?" she asked, eyeing me carefully. "I gotta get to Buena Vista. I got a check comin' to me at the post office up there. They'll send it back if I don't claim it soon."

This bit of news helped to explain her desperation for reaching her destination. "I promise," I said. I knew someone at the Gathering Place would have a better solution than hitchhiking. Maybe one of the staff would be able to drive her to the mountains. I had no strategy whatsoever. I just wanted to get Ruby, Lizzie Lou, and myself in the car with the heater cranked up to 90 degrees!

Lizzie Lou barked and snarled at me even more aggressively when I stood up to herd her toward the car. Her lip was curled, and her wiry hair was standing up on her neck. I began picking up Ruby's blanket and the other items strewn about the curb. Ruby gathered her cane and duffel bag. She packed up Lizzie Lou's bowl of food and emptied her water dish. She seemed pretty nonchalant about the fact that Lizzie Lou's leash was wound around my legs and her teeth were within striking distance of my bare ankles.

When we got to my car, I spread the blanket, coyote side up, in the back seat for Lizzie Lou. She would have no part of it and stayed on Ruby's lap in the front. She glared and yapped at me the entire fifteen minutes it took to drive to The Gathering Place.

"I been to them shelters. I don't like 'em." Ruby announced, breaking the silence.

"I bet this one is different than any you've been to before." I tried to reassure her, then added, "I've volunteered here for a long time, and they treat their clients with kindness and respect. The staff works very hard to make you feel welcome."

"It ain't the staff I don't like. It's all them women and their sad stories. I got my own troubles. I don't want to hear about theirs. Makes me too depressed."

"I know what you mean, but when I see how women and children are being fed and surrounded by a community that cares for them, it helps me feel hopeful and less depressed."

"Well I ain't stayin'. Remember your promise?"

By the time we pulled up to the shelter, I was more than eager for some relief from Lizzie Lou's bad attitude and Ruby's persistent reminders of my promise to take her back where I found her. I had to admit taking her back was starting to sound like a pretty good idea.

Ruby perked up when she saw a group of women standing outside the shelter in a cloud of smoke. I could tell from our short ride in my smoke-free car, that already smelled like an ashtray, she would like to join them in that cloud. Fortunately, God granted me the grace to be much less offended than I might have been if it had been a member of my family wreaking of smoke in my front seat. I could be a real Lizzie Lou when exposed to smoke! I swear I can smell it when someone lights up on television.

Ruby and Lizzie Lou slowly got out of the car and Ruby had me double-check that I locked the car doors, since we were leaving her things there. The three of us went inside to get advice and lunch. I quickly explained the situation to the shelter's intake manager, Dottie. She helped Ruby and Lizzie Lou get settled on the sheltered smoking porch with a bowl of food and water for Lizzie Lou and a warm lunch for Ruby.

I excused myself while Ruby ate so I could speak with Dottie about ideas to help Ruby get to Buena Vista. Dottie reluctantly explained that no one was going to the mountains and no bus would take Ruby with the dog. Of course, a wise woman had already warned me that buses don't allow dogs, but I needed further confirmation.

Dottie and I decided it would be best for Ruby to get a decent night's rest. (She'd slept on a cold bench at a truck stop the night before.) It was late afternoon, and I wasn't about to take her back to where I had found her, regardless of the promises I made earlier.

I went out to the porch to check on Ruby. She was eating her lunch and chatting with a couple of the other women. I sat with them for a while and listened as they talked about the weather and what arrangements they had for shelter that evening. The Gathering Place is a daytime shelter only. I looked around at this place I had grown familiar with over the years.

THE FIRST TIME I'd visited the Gathering Place, was when it was located in an old vacant store front. There were just a few clients. I went with Cheri, a friend from my church, to take a tour and learn more about the shelter for women and children. At the time they served about twenty-five women a day by offering warmth, protection from the streets, and a nutritious meal. The first person I saw upon entering the front door of the one-room facility on Santa Fe Drive was a homeless toddler asleep on a worn sofa, covered by a thin, tattered blanket.

I stared. The little girl was about the age of my daughter. Unprepared for this reality, I excused myself and walked right back out the door. I didn't want anyone to see me crying, so I walked around the corner and took deep breaths to calm myself. Cheri noticed my quick departure and came to comfort me. I couldn't catch my breath, still thinking about the child on that couch. Where would this little one sleep tonight? Would she be warm enough? Would she go to sleep hungry?

I'd gone home that evening and told my husband about my experience. I was still nearly paralyzed with worry for the little girl, and Bruce suggested I not go back again. "It is too hard on you when you expose yourself to these things," He consoled. "I know you will obsess about this for days, Cy."

"I'm going back. I signed up to drive a family to the new facility, to show them where they will go in a couple of weeks." I told him that turning my back wouldn't help anyone. I explained that probably everyone who volunteers feels over-whelmed at first but the temporary discomfort and sorrow can be an inspiration to bring hope to a woman or child whose discomfort is most likely not temporary.

A few weeks later I drove a family from that very meager shelter to the spacious new building. Several volunteers were taking families to show them where the new Gathering Place would be located and help them learn how to get there by bus or foot from the old location. It was important they not feel abandoned when the old shelter closed its doors. I wrote the first article I ever published about that experience. It was called "A Warm Day in December" and was published by the *Denver Post*. It began: "Today I didn't read about the homeless or watch the homeless standing in a food line. Today I held the homeless in my arms, and I will never be the same."

The family assigned to my car that day consisted of a mother, who was deaf, and her three little boys, ages six, four, and eighteen months. It was a warm December afternoon, but the three boys were all bundled up and eager for this adventurous trip to the new Gathering Place. I buckled the little one in my daughter's car seat. She was at the Mommy's Day Out program at our church, so her seat was conveniently vacant for a few hours. The older boys were having fun pushing the electric window buttons up and down. Their mom, sitting in the front with me, would snap her fingers and give them a few "I'm warning you" looks. I thought their wonder was delightful as they oohed and aahed over the Christmas decorations outside the "magic" windows. The baby, however, looked like he was coming down with a cold or flu. His cheeks looked flushed and he was lethargic.

We arrived at the Gathering Places' new building on Fifteenth and High Streets. I parked in their small lot and unbuckled the older boys before lifting the baby from his car seat. He felt feverish to me. Since it was such an unusually warm day in December, I suggested they leave their heavy, threadbare coats in my car. Everyone resisted my attempts to free them from their jackets. Suddenly I realized why. They had been conditioned to never leave their coats anywhere. Just because they were uncomfortably warm was not a good reason to risk not having their coats in a few hours when the sun went behind the clouds. They knew what it felt like to be painfully cold. Unlike my children, these three little boys had no closet; they had no home.

It was that experience that made me want to step out of my comfort zone in my Littleton suburb and tread where I had never been. Thankfully, I would never be the same.

Now, here I was ten years later, sitting with Ruby on the patio of this same facility. God was reminding me He always has a plan, and he gives us a choice to be a part of it. I just needed to let my feelings of insecurity go and trust Him.

I went back to speak with Dottie about what I should do. "Do not to get too personally involved with the clients," she told me. It was a typical refrain around the Gathering Place. Today was no exception as Dottie reminded me of another occasion when I had followed my heart instead of my head.

One time I was gently chastised after someone witnessed me sharing my lipstick with a Gathering Place client. I'd spent time with this client before. I knew she had been a prostitute, but I admired her courage to change her lifestyle and seek a better life for her child and herself. We'd had conversations about our two-year-old daughters and traded stories about the exasperation and joy of parenting. We had become friends, and were in the lady's room freshening up. My friend was about to share her testimony with a group of volunteers. She was upset about forgetting her lipstick, so I let her borrow mine. Apparently, this was not considered a "safe" thing to do.

Now, my involvement with Ruby was setting off warning bells, and Dottie's was concerned I was getting too close. I told her not to worry about me, that I wasn't going to get too involved. I simply felt God wanted me to get Ruby to a warm, safe place for the night.

Dottie suggested that Ruby use one of the vouchers donated to the Gathering Place for a nearby motel where she could spend the night. Dottie and I agreed to talk again in the morning about how to get Ruby to Buena Vista.

On my way back to the smoking porch to find Ruby, I looked at the clock.

Oh my gosh! I thought. I needed to pick up my daughter, now in the seventh grade, from school in the next half hour. I hurried back inside to find Dottie.

"Dottie, can you get the voucher ready and check to see if a room is available? I have to pick up my daughter at school. It will take me about forty-five minutes to get back here and then I'll explain the motel thing to Ruby."

I went back out to the porch where Ruby was still enjoying lunch and told her I was going to leave for a few minutes.

"You promised you was going to take me back to where you found me!" Ruby said, practically in a state of panic.

"I know, Ruby, but I have to pick up my daughter. She will be waiting for me when school gets out. Trust me, she doesn't like to wait. This way, you will be able to finish your lunch and relax for a few minutes. I'll be back really soon, and we will talk about what to do next." I tried to convince her.

"You promise?"

"Yes, I promise. I'll be right back."

TWO

You Came Back!

I arrived at Whitney's school and, thankfully, she was out in front waiting for me. There was a slight glitch: she had offered her friend Kendra a ride home. On the way back to the shelter I gave the girls a Cliffs Notes version of the extraordinary events that had occurred since Whitney left for school earlier that morning. They were thrilled to be transported from a boring, uneventful day at middle school to a real-life drama. They couldn't wait to meet the homeless lady! Even better, she had a dog. Little did they know.

I called Kendra's mom, Christy, who was in Bible study with me that morning and brought her up to speed. "Remember the homeless lady we prayed for today? I can fill you in later, but I'm just going to take her to a motel and then I'll head home with the girls and drop Kendra at your house. Is that alright with you?"

Whitney and Kendra were full of questions, "What is the lady's name? Is she nice? What's her dog's name? Where is everyone going to sit? Is this her bag? Can we move it to the trunk? How come everything smells like smoke?"

When Whitney, Kendra and I pulled into the parking lot at the Gathering Place, Ruby was standing on the corner with Lizzie Lou in her arms, staring west, toward the mountains. She looked a bit better after having lunch, but my heart ached at the sight of her. She looked so exhausted. How can she still be standing? The gray braids hanging from the sides of her head melted my heart and at the same time made me smile. I assumed she must be about eighty with all the deep wrinkles, her cane, and gray hair.

"You came back!" she exclaimed as soon as she saw me. "Ain't nobody ever come back for me before!"

"Of course, I did, silly. I told you I would. This is my daughter, Whitney and her friend Kendra. Girls, this is Ruby."

"Nice to meet ya," Ruby responded with uncharacteristic politeness.

"You, too," they each replied.

Then one of the girls asked, "What's your dog's name?"

"Lizzie Lou, but her pedigree name is Elizabeth Louise."

Oh, now I get the attitude, I thought with a smile. *She has a pedigree.*

Dottie came out to meet us and handed me the motel voucher. She offered to call a cab to take Ruby to the motel, but I vetoed the idea. I wanted to drive her to the motel.

As we walked to my car, I calmly explained to Ruby about spending the night in a motel. I didn't explain it very well because the next thing I heard was, "I ain't goin' to no motel. You promised you was going to take me back to where you found me!" She was angry. I feared I had lost the trust I had recently gained.

"Ruby, it is getting late. It will be dark soon, and it is getting colder by the minute." Even though it was April, the air felt wet and cold. The temperature was dropping, and the dark clouds over the mountains looked like they might bring snow. "I am going to drive you to the motel and check you in. Then I will come back in the morning and take you to your spot by the road where I found you, if nothing else works out."

"I ain't got money for no motel."

"We have a voucher that will cover it." I reminded her.

"You'll get me back to my spot tomorrow morning? Early? Promise?" She was finally either too tired to argue or could sense I might be just as stubborn as she was.

"I promise."

I'd made more promises in the last few hours than on my wedding day.

"Girls get in the back, Ruby and Lizzie Lou are riding shotgun."

Lizzie Lou surprised me by jumping into the back seat with the girls. Actually, she seemed happy to have two more people to protect from me. She settled her scruffy little self between Whitney and Kendra. She never yapped a word at them. She really rubbed it in by laying her head in Whitney's lap. She kept me in her steely-eyed glare the minute I got behind the wheel. Clearly I was not making any headway with Elizabeth Louise.

As we pulled up to the motel, I was shocked. Seriously, this is it? I must have the wrong address. I double-checked. Nope, it was the right address.

Maybe they are remodeling the inside before starting on the outside.

Dream on, Pollyanna.

"Everyone wait in the car. Lock the doors after me, I'm going in to talk to the manager." I double-checked that the doors were locked and warily crept toward the office door. The office sign was dangling vertically on one nail. A man stood behind a counter cluttered with candy wrappers and Skol cans, reading something while leaning on his elbows. He appeared to be in charge.

"Excuse me, sir, the Gathering Place gave me a voucher for a room for my friend and her dog for tonight."

"Yeah?" he grunted.

"Yes," I waived the voucher at him, but he didn't look up from the riveting "article" in his men's magazine.

"You owe me forty-nine bucks for the room plus a fifteen-dollar deposit for the dog."

"No, I have a voucher, and I was told dogs were welcome at no extra charge." I explained.

"You was told wrong," he grunted, still engrossed by his reading material; he didn't bother to look up. He didn't seem impressed with my voucher, and I didn't foresee a good outcome by arguing.

"Will you take a check?"

"Yeah, whatever, but I need your license and one for the lady staying here."

It was easy to see this guy wasn't on the fast track up the corporate ladder.

Back at the car I knocked on the passenger-side window. Ruby rolled it down part way. I asked if she had a legal form of identification and was surprised when she handed me a valid Colorado ID.

"Lock her up. I'll be right back," I ordered. I was starting to get a little edgy. As I walked back in to begin another engaging conversation with my biggest fan, I looked at Ruby's birthdate on the ID: December 17, 1945. I looked again. Ruby wasn't eighty like I told the girls. In fact, she was just fifty-four, five years older than me.

I handed Norman Bates our identification documents and a check for sixty-four dollars. He painstakingly wrote several rows of numbers on the back of the check and repeatedly looked up at me, then at my ID, like an overzealous detective on a sitcom. I liked it better when he was consumed with his magazine.

I took the key and headed to the designated room around the corner. As it turned out there was no need for a key. The door was partially open. The bed was disheveled. There was a beer bottle on the floor and a Burger King sack on the nightstand.

One very angry woman did an about-face and marched back to the manager's office with her hair on fire. "Give me that check!" I demanded. He was still holding it when I yanked it from his grimy grip.

"Do you seriously think you have any right to take money from anyone for that pit? It is filthy, the door has a hole in it; there's leftover trash everywhere! My friend will not be staying in that room tonight or ever! I'm reporting this establishment to . . . to . . . well, to someone who should know about it!"

I stomped off praying I would make it to the car without being followed. Of course, that would have required physical effort on Norman's part, so there was probably no need for concern.

Still, I banged on the car window to be let in like a victim of a Freddy Krueger movie. I told Ruby and the girls that the room wasn't available after all. This seemed like welcome news to them, as they were not impressed with the place. Ruby thanked me for not making her stay there and asked me for the millionth time to take her back to where I found her.

"Nope, that isn't happening." I headed south toward my area of town and told her we would look for other motels. I sped by all of the signs facing the highway.

No vacancy. No pets. No way.

"Okay, that's it. Ruby Jean you're coming home with Whitney and me. Kendra, call your mom and ask her if she can pick you up at our house."

THREE

Hi Honey, Guess What?

---

*A*fter debating me for five minutes, Ruby relented. She probably realized she was in a hostage situation. After all, I had the car, her dog, and all her worldly belongings going seventy miles per hour down I-25 toward Lone Tree, Colorado.

On the way I called my husband at his office to give him a heads-up.

"Hi, honey, guess what? We are going to have an overnight guest this evening."

"Who?" he asked. Bruce sounded preoccupied, he was probably doing his lawyer stuff and reviewing a document when I interrupted him.

"I just met her. She's in the car with Whitney and me." I have a knack for getting his attention. I didn't tell him about the "homeless" part yet, because I didn't want Ruby to hear me labeling her.

He quickly became fully engaged, and the interrogation began. "You just met her? Where??"

"We met outside of my Bible study today," I said, using my matter-of-fact tone of voice.

"You just met her, and she is spending the night? At our house? Cy, what have you gotten yourself into this time?" He sounded like Ricky Riccardo from *I Love Lucy*.

Lucy: "She's looking forward to meeting you too. I love you. Bye."

When Bruce walked in the front door after his long day at work and lengthy commute he found Whitney, Ruby, *and Lizzie Lou* on the couch. (Quincy, our dog, was sulking in the corner since she wasn't allowed on the new furniture and apparently Lizzy was.) Whitney was teaching Ruby how to play Nintendo.

Lizzie Lou, quick to spot an intruder, flew off the couch and began barking at Bruce, circling and nipping at his ankles. Leave it to Lizzie Lou to make a good impression.

"Hi, honey," I said cheerfully, hoping to run interference. "Um, this is Ruby, my new friend I told you about . . . and Lizzie Lou." I was really pouring on the "honey" thing.

"Lizzie Lou! Lizzie Lou! You hush up!" Ruby scolded over the shrill barking.

Ever the gentleman, Bruce introduced himself and welcomed Ruby. He tried his best to make her feel comfortable. But if she didn't trust me, she sure didn't trust this six-foot-three man in a suit and tie who was wielding a briefcase as a shield against Lizzie Lou's fencing moves: advance, nip, retreat, repeat. Bruce looked beseechingly at Whitney, who just shrugged her shoulders and rolled her eyes at me.

"Nice to meet you." Ruby mumbled, sort of offering a hand for Bruce to shake. "Cy, you got anywhere I could wash up? She was visibly uncomfortable, and I knew she wanted to escape— as did poor Bruce.

"Of course, but it's upstairs. Can you make it alright?" I asked of a woman who had been hitchhiking for days and planned to walk to the mountains if she had to. Fourteen stairs probably didn't intimidate her.

Still, I followed behind her up the stairs with my hands outstretched to break her fall just in case. We walked down the hallway to the guest room. She stepped gingerly in the room and peeked in the bathroom. "I see you got a shower in there. Think I could rinse off?" she asked shyly.

"Sure, I'll call you when dinner is ready. Just make yourself at home. Clean towels are on the towel bar, and there's soap in the shower."

While Ruby took a long, hot shower, I put one of my robes on her bed and tossed her clothes and blanket in the washer. I figured she wouldn't mind.

Later, when I didn't hear the water running anymore, I knocked on her door to invite her down to dinner. When she didn't answer, I gingerly opened the door and saw she was asleep in my bathrobe on top of the covers. Her wet hair was wrapped in a towel like a turban. It almost seemed as if some of her wrinkles had melted away as she slept. Later, I took a dinner tray up to her room. I told her to get under the covers and said, "We are so happy you decided to stay here for the night, Ruby. Sleep well. I'll see you in the morning."

"Good night, Cy. Thank your husband and Whitney for letting me stay."

Lizzie Lou seemed content on the pillow next to Ruby.

"Good night, Lizzie Lou." I pulled the door closed gently behind me. I had my first sense of peace the entire day knowing our guests were safe and warm.

When Bruce and I went to bed, I filled him in on my plans for a road trip the next day and assured him that I would be safe and home in time for him to take me out to dinner.

He told me it was a nice thing I had done and he was proud

of me. Oh, and he said something to the effect of how I was going to be the death of him.

"Good night, Ricky."

FOUR

You Ever Heard of Oprah?

he next morning something miraculous happened. Lizzie Lou didn't bark at me. I almost barked at her, though, as payback for the day before. Bruce, regrettably, had not been allowed into the "circle of trust." Over Lizzie Lou's yapping and growling, he told Ruby goodbye and thanked her for staying with us.

"Thank you, sir." she replied, still as wary as Lizzie Lou.

When Whitney hugged her goodbye, Ruby thanked her for teaching her "Intendo."

"I'm gonna get me one of them someday," she added. "'Course, gotta get me a TV first."

I gave Whit and Bruce cheek-kisses goodbye and tried to act like they were witnessing a normal morning, rather than two improbable cohorts getting ready to take off on day two of their Odd Couple adventure. Ruby had her to-go coffee. I had my to-go iced tea, and Lizzie Lou had her to-go bowl of Mighty Dog.

Truthfully, I was feeling kind of anxious about the three plus hour drive since Ruby and I hadn't really talked that much the day before. I didn't know how much to ask without making her feel that I was prying, and I wasn't sure I had anything to say that would be of interest to her. Did we have anything at all in common?

As soon as we hit the freeway, I started filling in the silence with my nervous chatter. Ruby was quiet and let me ramble on for the first part of the trip. Thank goodness I am an accomplished rambler.

We stopped for a few smoke breaks, which took a while because she rolled her own cigarettes. Ruby proclaimed that rolling her own was not only cheaper but far healthier, because that made them more "natural." I stared at her in wide-eyed disbelief, thinking, *Don't get me started.*

Between the rolling and then smoking each cigarette to the very end (she didn't want to let a single puff go to waste) we weren't making the best time.

Unfortunately, Lizzie Lou's bathroom breaks didn't coordinate with Ruby's smoke breaks. Shortly after one of Ruby's smoke breaks the demanding terrier went berserk when we were on a winding mountain road with large trucks thundering past. She scratched at the window like a maniac until I pulled over. Ruby hovered by the side of the busy highway tethered to Lizzie Lou as the cantankerous canine circled, sniffed, and circled some more for just the right spot. I remained in the car as other vehicles roared by within inches of the car's side mirror.

"Elizabeth Louise! You are going to be the death of me!" Ruby scolded. Familiar words since Bruce just said them to me the night before—in this case they may be prophetic.

Eventually, Ruby started to engage in conversation, and I began to get a glimpse of a life I could not imagine.

She talked about the "little brother" she was trying to visit.

She said how much she loved him and how he had been wrongfully convicted.

"I sat in that courtroom every single day," she explained. "They didn't even get him a real lawyer. He was court appointed 'cause my brother didn't have no money. I found out it was that lawyer's first case. He hadn't ever defended no one before! He told my brother to plead guilty, and they'd go easy on him. I begged him not to plead guilty since he wasn't guilty. He listened to that lawyer, and they gave him a life sentence." She looked and sounded as angry as if the judge had just pounded the gavel.

"He was always such a sweet boy," she told me. "Didn't do nothin' to hurt nobody. He was kind, hardworking . . . always trying to help others out."

Then she said, "When I was about seven years old, my mother left me to watch my two-year-old brother. She said she'd be back in a while, but after several days a neighbor musta called one of them child protection places. Them people came to the door, and without any warning they took my baby brother out of his high chair and put him in the back seat of a car parked out on the road in front of our trailer. He was crying and callin' for me. They kept saying he'd be cared for. Hell, I mean heck, I was carin' for him just fine. They split us up."

"What happened then?" I asked.

She admitted she didn't know what happened to him. "They sent me to live with a Mormon family that fostered kids in Utah. They didn't love me, but they fed me and got me to school. I loved learnin' my letters and numbers," she remembered with a wistful smile.

After Ruby had been living with the foster family a few years, her mother came to visit. She convinced Ruby to leave the security of her surroundings and travel with her to California on a bus. "She made me think she had a place for me to live out there in California," Ruby told me matter-of-factly. "She said she missed me. I shouldn't have trusted her."

As I listened, I thought it was unlikely that Ruby could simply walk out of foster care, and I wondered if she had been kidnapped by her own mother. But I didn't interrupt her story to ask as she was finally opening up to me.

"Turns out she just needed me to work the fields, pickin' grapes, so she'd have money for her booze. I wasn't very big, but they worked me hard. My hands were all cut up by the end of the day."

We rode in silence for a while as I absorbed the appalling circumstances that the woman riding next to me had suffered. My eyes started to water when she blurted out, "I was raped for the first time when I was about thirteen." I didn't even have a moment to respond before she revealed more. "Coupla years later I met me what I thought was a really nice man. I was sure he actually cared for me. At least until after I had his baby."

"How old were you then?"

"I was fifteen. He was older. His family said I wasn't good enough for him or to mother *his* baby. They came and took my child right out of the hospital. He had me sign some paper. They told me it was the baby's birth certificate." She was staring out the passenger window, and I had to strain to hear her. "I guess it was me signing away my baby. I never even got to hold my baby girl."

"Oh, Ruby, I am so sorry. I know you would have been a wonderful mother." I reached over to pat her shoulder.

"I sure would have loved that baby. I still think of her. She's probably a mother herself. I might even have me some grand-kids. Don't matter, I ain't ever gonna know. They just took her, leavin' me to wonder the rest of my life. Can we stop for a smoke?"

While she stood on the side of the road smoking, I had time to think about what she'd just told me. At fifteen, Ruby was frightened, bullied, and alone. She was left to agonize over so many unanswered questions: Was her daughter well? Was she being raised by a mother who loved her? Did she look like Ruby? My new friend had clearly suffered too much.

When Ruby got back into the car, I shared with her my personal anguish over having babies in heaven I never got to hold. I hoped it would make her feel less alone in her suffering. We suffered in two different sets of circumstances, but we were still two mothers with holes in our hearts. Threads don't get more common than those of grieving mothers. We expressed our sympathy for one another, and the vast space between our lives began to close.

Ruby went on to tell me about marrying a man who was very abusive. Ruby left him after living too many years with his cruelty. "He was a mean son of a bitch. Sorry to cuss in front of you, but ain't no other way to describe him. I done his cookin' and cleanin'. He was a nasty old drunk and liked to knock me around. I done too much drinkin' then, too," she confessed.

After leaving him, Ruby was homeless off and on, employed off and on.

"Lived here and there," was the way she put it.

The only job she mentioned was working at a nursing home for a while. "I loved them old people, but they laid me off—never said why."

As we wound through her story and the curves of the mountain she circled back to her brother.

"He was convicted of a murder he had nothin' to do with. Them boys he was hanging out with tricked him and framed him. He thought they was taking him to a job site so he could get him some work. He shoulda known better than to trust them. They were no good. He was a bad drinker in them days." She went onto explain that her brother was passed out in the car when he was arrested, and that the men who had "given him a ride" had actually killed a man.

"My brother didn't know what was happening when they threw him in jail," Ruby told me, adding that she would stake her life on his innocence.

To me, it sounded as though she *had* staked her life on him. Every day since his conviction Ruby had devoted her time, energy, and meager means trying to find someone to take up his case and appeal what she believed was his wrongful incarceration. He'd been in prison for nineteen years. She'd been imprisoned by loneliness and despair during those same nineteen years, trying her best to survive on her own.

For several miles we sat in silence. I was thinking about Ruby's revelations when she broke the quiet by asking: "You ever heard of Oprah?"

Oprah? How did we get on Oprah? I wondered before answering her question. "Sure, I've watched her show a few times. But I don't really watch a lot of television in the daytime," I said apologetically as if not being a daily follower of Oprah might be offensive to her.

"Well, I figure her to be a pretty nice person, but I don't think she's ever taken a stranger home to spend the night and take a shower at her place."

I burst out laughing, so Ruby started to laugh. I told her I loved her laugh. She said no one ever told her that before. She added, "I ain't ever laughed much, though." She continued on her Oprah revelry: "I ain't kiddin'. Oprah gives out some nice prizes on her TV show. I'd sure like to get in her audience."

Then she said something that would have drawn gales of laughter from my family.

"I been wondering if you ain't some kinda angel."

A moment later she apologized again for using a few cuss words during our drive. "I shoulda' known better since I met you comin' outta that church. You're a Christian, right?"

"Yes, I am. Actually, I don't know what I would do if I didn't have Jesus in my life. I hope you know He is in your life, too. He is the reason why we are in this car together."

I was profoundly aware that Jesus was the only explanation for the implausible relationship growing between Ruby and me.

"Well, I imagine there's some good ones like you, but I seen them preachers on TV, the ones that want all your money. I used to try and send this one preacher a little bit whenever I could. I thought it might help my brother. Then him and his wife ended up in jail!" she exclaimed indignantly. "I run into plenty of people who call themselves Christians. They might give you five bucks to make themselves feel good, but then they go on their way, thinkin' they done their good deed for the day," she said, painting with a wide brush.

"Ruby, I've done that before," I said. "I've given five dollars to someone who is holding a sign on a corner. Sometimes we just don't know what to do to help someone. For all you know, those people who gave you the five dollars said a little prayer for you as they drove away."

FIVE

Lunch with a Side of Jesus and Jelly

*W*e drove a little further, and I spotted a cute looking roadside cafe.

"This looks nice. Let's stop there for lunch," I said, pointing it out to Ruby. I was already pulling into the parking lot.

"This place is too nice. Just bring me something out to the car. I ain't even that hungry. Besides, I ain't dressed for no fancy restaurant."

"Ruby, it's not fancy. It looks kind of homey. Let's just go in and check it out."

Ruby reached for the door handle, giving in more quickly than usual. She was either hungrier than she was letting on, or she knew I would eventually get my way.

The hostess greeted us with a smile. "Welcome! How are you two pretty ladies today?"

Thank you, Lord, that was just the greeting we needed.

Ruby asked directions to the restroom so she could wash her hands before we sat down. I joined her. When we came back, she sat in the booth and opened the menu. I saw a troubled look developing on her face. "I don't like the stuff that comes with what I want. Besides, these prices are too high."

When the waitress came to take our order, I winked at her and said, "I was just telling my friend, Ruby, that I bet you let people pick whatever they want for sides after they choose the main dish they would like. I'm sure there is no extra charge."

Ruby didn't see the wink, and thankfully our waitress embraced the conspiracy. "That's right, just tell me what you want, honey, and I'll make it happen."

Ruby's appetite obviously improved with that news, because she ordered a stack of pancakes, two eggs over-easy, white toast, a bowl of chili, hash browns, a cup of coffee, and a large milk. Then she added a hot fudge sundae from the kid's menu. "Can you bring that ice cream out after I'm done? I'll want a refill on my coffee by then. Does that sundae come with whipped cream?"

A girl after my own heart.

I closed my menu and smiled at our waitress. "I'll have a cobb salad and sundae too—with extra whipped cream, please!"

LUNCH WAS NEARLY A TWO-HOUR AFFAIR. As we chatted, I was able to segue into the reason I felt she and I met the day before.

"Ruby, it wasn't me who picked you up yesterday; it was Jesus. My Bible study friends prayed for you. They asked God to provide someone to help you." I told her I was *not* an angel but that Jesus had indeed answered our group's prayer. Jesus wanted me to be the *someone* we had asked him to provide. "Ruby," I said, "Jesus loves you so much—"

"I ain't loveable," she interrupted. "If you knew all about me, you would never have picked me up." she declared.

"Listen, Ruby, if you knew all about me, you would never have gotten in my car!" I countered.

"You're kinda funny, Cy."

"Finally! I've been trying to tell you that all along. I even wrote a humor book a few years ago. I'll give you a copy."

"Nah, that's ok. I don't like them books where people think they're funny. They ain't that funny to me."

"Well, who knows, maybe you'll think this one's funny since you know the author," I teased.

"What's it about? How to pick up strangers?"

"Exactly, because when I do, so few live to tell about it," I deadpanned.

"See, that ain't funny."

"Okay then, let's get back to why I think we are together this minute."

I told her God knows all about both of us, and He put us in one another's life for a purpose. I was pretty sure my purpose was to tell her about Jesus and lead her to accepting Him as her friend and Savior if she hadn't already. And if she did believe, God wanted to remind her He was watching over her.

Then I told her I was pretty sure her purpose in my life was to teach me to serve. "I've studied the Bible a long time, Ruby, I think God wants to see what I've learned."

"I've tried readin' it, but it didn't make no sense. I always believed there is a God. I just ain't sure what to believe about him. I used to tell my brother about God. Told him he could trust God to take care of him if I couldn't."

"You need to believe He loves you, believe He knows you, believe He sent his Son to die for you, believe He died for your sins, believe He is alive. Have faith in Him, Ruby."

"I try, but I ain't seen no sign of Him in my brother's life or mine. In parts of the Bible I did read, God's so mean. Letting

His own Son die? That's what I don't understand. How could He let that happen? That don't sound like a very loving father. I don't have much faith in nobody anymore." She was closing down this conversation.

Nothing I'd said seemed to have made a difference. I prayed silently, *God, why didn't you give me the right words to say when I had the opportunity? Was I not listening to You?*

When our sundaes and Ruby's coffee refill arrived, she asked for several to-go boxes and painstakingly placed her leftovers in three different containers. Just before leaving the table, she dumped all the Smucker's jellies from the little wire container on the table into her handbag. She looked at me through her enormous, thick, tinted, duct-taped bifocals with total sincerity and said, "I heard once on Oprah or Dr. Phil or somewhere that them jellies, salt and pepper, and sugar are figured into your bill, so you should always take 'em!"

When Ruby wasn't looking, I put ten dollars on the table to cover our jelly larceny.

At last, we reached Buena Vista. Prison visiting hours didn't start until the next day, so I asked her about her plans. "Do you have somewhere to stay up here?"

"Oh, I know people in these parts. I've stayed up here before. Even lived here for a while, so I could visit my brother."

"Do you need to call someone you know and tell them you need a place to stay?" I inquired.

"Nah, I like sleeping in the park."

"What am I going to do with you?" I chided.

I checked her into a small motel and paid for a week's rent to ease my mind. Just across the street was a grocery store, so we loaded a Styrofoam cooler with some food for

Ruby and Lizzie Lou. She assured me she would be in touch with friends who would take her in. "Don't you worry, Cy. You already done enough for me. I ain't never gonna forget it."

Back at the motel, she seemed delighted by the clean room and comfortable bed. (It deserved five stars compared to our last experience.) She put Lizzie Lou's food and water bowl by the bed and turned back the covers. We both had a long and emotional day. I knew she would fall asleep in a safe, clean room. And while my heart was happy for this reprieve for Ruby, I was worried about her future.

When I leaned in to hug her goodbye, she acted awkward and kept her arms to her sides.

I wrote my phone number on a piece of paper and asked her to call if she ever needed anything.

"I'll be fine, you got me all set up here. I'll call my friends in the morning," she assured me.

I walked to my car completely exhausted from the unexpected turn of the past two days. I had been running on the Holy Spirit and adrenaline. I felt truly blessed to have met Ruby, but I also felt I wasn't leaving her in much better shape than when we first met by the curb. I hadn't done a very good job of sharing Christ with her. I certainly didn't answer her questions. At best I'd given her a couple of days of warmth and shelter. Was that all God was asking of me?

I was opening the car door to start my downhill drive toward home when I heard her voice.

"Cy, wait!"

Oh no, now what? I was so exhausted, I selfishly just wanted to get on my way home.

"Would you please call me when you get home, so I know you are safe? And don't go pickin' up no strangers!"

I thanked her for her concern and promised I would call, adding, "And lock your door, by the way!"

Climbing into my car, I heard her call out again from her open motel room door.

"Cy, I'll always love you even if I never see you again."

"I hope we will see one another again. I love you, too, Ruby."

Heading back down the mountain, I could barely see where I was driving. Tears that had just blurred my vision earlier now caused me to pull over and try to collect myself.

SIX

I'll Be Coming Down the Mountain with My Mom

---

*M*y mom had been in heaven almost a year. I missed hugging her. And I missed hearing her voice during our regular Sunday afternoon phone calls. And yet our conversations still seemed loud and clear to me. In fact, on my drive down the mountain after leaving Ruby, I could almost hear my mother's voice: *"Oh, Cy, I'm so glad you picked up Ruby and Lizzie Lou today. Can you imagine them hitchhiking in the cold all the way to Buena Vista? No telling who might have picked them up! Or maybe no one . . . then what? You did the right thing, honey."*

I'd been thinking a lot about my mom since I'd met Ruby.

She would have loved every minute of the last thirty hours. She probably would have insisted on sitting in the back with Lizzie Lou cuddled on her lap. Lizzie Lou would have loved her, too. If dogs purred, that's what Lizzie Lou would have been doing.

As I navigated a curve on the highway, I started talking to her. I don't know if she could hear me, but I like to think she heard every word.

———

Mom, I've been thinking about you ever since I met Ruby yesterday. It has never been clearer how blessed I was to have you as my mentor and my mother. Truly, Mom, I want to thank you for the example you set for me my whole life. You were a living illustration of mercy. I remember so many times I watched you give graciously and generously to someone in need. I grew up thinking this was the natural order of things. You had such a servant's heart.

You always had a sixth sense for discerning the needs of others. When I think about your generous spirit, I often remember the time we went ice-skating on a pond in Mineral Palace Park in Pueblo where I grew up. I must have been about ten years old. That was the morning you suddenly announced, "I'm declaring today a chore-free Saturday!" (I was so relieved, since being the youngest—and the closest to the ground—my weekly chore was dusting all the table legs). Then you said, "Today, I am going to teach you to ice skate!"

I was all in. In fact, images of the Olympics hovered over me like a thought bubble. But after rustling around in some cardboard box in our musty, creepy basement, you pulled out a pair of old, brown hand-me-down skates. I was so disappointed!

I remembered thinking that Peggy Fleming wouldn't have been caught dead in these old brown skates. They were nothing at all like the beautiful white ice skates I'd always longed to wear. Besides, I wanted to look good on my first triple salchow. Oh, how I pouted in the car as you drove us to the lake. I was so focused on the sorry state of my skates, I was the epitome of an ungrateful kid.

Now that I think about it, you should have canceled my

skating lessons on the spot. But you soldiered on, immune to my theatrics.

Even now, I'm smiling at the memory.

As soon as I was on the lake, I discovered that standing up on my skates for more than two minutes was a lot harder than I imagined. Of course, I blamed the hideous color of my skates for my lack of proficiency.

I continued to whine about how much I hated my skates every time I fell, and after about a half hour, you told me to take off my skates. I assumed you'd grown tired of my whining. (I was tired of my whining too, but I was committed to it!) I remember wondering if you were taking me home and reluctantly admitted to myself that maybe I'd overplayed it.

But that's when you said, "We'll come right back. We just have a little errand to run."

We drove to the nearby mall, and I sat in the car with the heater running while you went in to Sears for something. And when you came out, you had a big bag.

I remember thinking, *I'll bet the bag has my new white skates in it! Great! All my whining paid off after all!*

We drove back to the pond, and I tramped through the snow drifts, without a single complaint, down toward the ice. My mood had lifted appreciably in anticipation of gliding across the ice on my shiny new blades. And then you stopped at a bench where a young girl I knew from school was sitting. Anna was bundled up with her shoulders hunched up around her bright red uncovered ears, her hands jammed in the pockets of her brown cloth coat.

"Hi, honey. I think you know Cy from school," you said. "We saw you sitting here and thought you might like to join our skating lesson. I hope these fit. We would like you to have them."

That's when you opened the Sears bag and gave her a box. Inside that box was a pair of brand-new white skates.

Anna's red face grew redder and brighter. The bag also contained a pink hat with a white pom-pom and a pair of matching gloves.

"These are for me?" she asked, stunned. "To keep?"

Curiously, I didn't feel envious.

"Yes, to keep," you told her. "I think Cy would have more fun if she had someone to learn alongside."

I remember you told me, "Cy, put your skates back on, and you and Anna show this pond a thing or two."

You had quietly observed her longing to join in. I know you recognized her as a little girl from my class. Her parents spoke broken English, and their daughter had trouble making friends at school. I felt such an uplifting of my spirit as I helped Anna tie her new skates. I wasn't jealous of her good fortune at all. In fact, I was so proud I had a mother like you. I was generally very solicitous of your undivided attention, but I was actually delighted to share you as you walked Anna and me out to the ice, holding our hands.

REMEMBER OUR PRECOCIOUS NEXT-DOOR NEIGHBOR, Tommy, Mom? He was friendless because most parents in the neighborhood kept their perfect progenies from playing with him because they didn't want his proclivity for mischief to "rub off" on them. I remember he was tall and awkward for a seven- or eight-year-old.

But unlike most adults, Mom, you always had a kind word for Tommy. You would purposely go outside to say hi to him over our back fence and draw him into a conversation. For some reason you found his antics—and even his swearing—

kind of amusing (despite the fact that you were *not* equally amused when such antics were employed by your own children, I must add).

You even invited Tommy over for cookies, checkers, and chats. It pains me now to admit that I usually found a reason to hide out in my room, practicing my ballet or playing with my dolls, during these soirees. The truth is I was mortified by the idea of befriending Tommy even though he was in my class at school. I realize now that you saw past all his peculiarities and recognized a lonesome kid. In retrospect I was a "mean girl."

Eventually, you had to set some boundaries with Tommy as he loved ringing our doorbell as much as he loved our cookies, and soon he was visiting with inconvenient frequency. Quick to find a creative solution, you told him you would put that ugly ceramic rooster in our kitchen window, which he could see from his kitchen. You explained that when the rooster was on the window sill, it was a signal that Tommy could come over and walk right in without even having to ring the doorbell.

As I recall, this worked fairly well until you had an unexpected two-week hospital stay. After you were home a day or two, he rang the doorbell with unrelenting ferocity. When you finally answered the door, there was Tommy.

"Missuth Gulick," he said, getting right to the point. "When are you going to put that *%#!&! rooster back in the window?"

You apologized profusely, and after that dressing down, the rooster began appearing in the kitchen window at least one or two days a week.

Mom, how many times have we laughed about Tommy and the rooster?

. . .

AND MOM, I also recall that our house always had an eccentric relative living with us. There was three-hundred-pound Aunt Georgia, who rarely left her chair. Then there was Great Aunt Mary, who suffering dementia and rarely sat her lithe little body down unless *Lassie* was on TV. Rounding out the group was Grandmother Mitchell, who loved a hot toddy and a game of Canasta. She was frail of body but that didn't slow her mind down one bit. Your Mom was a spunky, funny, older version of you. Even my friends loved to come over just to hang out with her—even though it meant they might bump into Aunt Georgia.

THEN THERE WERE the stray pets; dozens of dogs or cats turned up on our doorstep over the years. It was as though our address were written on some fire hydrant, "Want a nice hot meal and bed for the night? Here's the place to go." I always wanted to keep those misplaced pets, but you convinced me that they had owners who would miss them. You posted their descriptions in the lost and found section of the newspaper and called the local radio station to report our latest find on their animal segment featuring lost and found pets.

I vividly remember the time we unexpectedly found ourselves on the "lost" side of the equation. Our dog Amber ran away during a thunderstorm. She dug out under the fence before we could get home and bring her inside. We scoured the neighborhood for her. You drove down every street and alley calling her name. You called the newspaper and radio station seeking help in finding our beloved, aging spaniel. Every night for a week we sat around conjecturing how Amber might be faring. Was she freezing? Had she been hit by a car? Had someone found her? Finally, we received a call. The woman on the phone said she believed her family might have our dog. The caller reported the dog was doing well, and we could come get her whenever it was convenient.

Virginia, Greg, and I eagerly jumped in the car, and drove to the house about four miles away. The nice lady we'd spoken to on the phone answered the door and invited us all in.

"Honey, is this your dog?" she looked at me, and I could tell she hoped it wasn't.

"That's her!" I squealed, "Thank you so much for finding her!" I wanted to run right over to Amber, but for some reason I stayed put. She didn't run to me either. She was lying at the feet of a teenage girl tinkering at the piano.

"Alice loves her," the woman told us. "Your dog follows her everywhere."

I took a second glance at Alice and realized she was blind.

Mom, I vividly remember you walked over and sat on the piano bench next to Alice. Amber sat up and wagged her tail but scooted closer to Alice and rested her head on her lap. Alice bent down and kissed our often-crotchety old dog on the top of her head. You then got up and pulled Virginia, Greg, and me aside and asked if we were willing to part with Amber and let her spend her last few years with her new friend. I knew you were truly leaving the choice to us, and it had to be unanimous. A glance back at Amber and Alice solidified the answer for all of us.

When we walked back into the living room, Greg spoke first. "My sisters and I would like to know if you would like to have Amber," he declared to Alice's mother.

I will never forget her face.

She burst out crying.

"Oh, yes, thank you, thank you! We have not seen Alice so

calm and content before your sweet dog showed up on our front porch."

You thanked Alice for taking such good care of Amber and said, "She is your dog, now, Alice. Love each other well."

We all hugged Alice, her mom, and Amber goodbye. It was a tearful departure.

Thank you for trusting us, Mom, to make the right decision.

I OFTEN THINK of your many favorite quotes taped on the refrigerator door.

The saying "I complained because I had no shoes, until I met a man who had no feet" was displayed in several places around the house. Needless to say, you did not abide complaining. "I have nothing to wear," was never well received. Boredom was also unfathomable to you. You were never idle. Even when watching television, you crocheted, worked on crossword puzzles, or wrote in your poetry journal. That magical book was always handy, tucked on the second shelf of the table by your chair.

EVERY CHRISTMAS, Mom, when I am up late wrapping gifts, my heart is filled with memories of all those December nights when you sat at the dining room table with your black Singer sewing machine singing long after we had all gone to bed.

One memory that stands out to me above all others is the Christmas you were making bathrobes with matching stuffed animals for all of your grandkids. You embroidered each child's favorite animal on the pocket of the terry cloth robe. When those were done, you created, without a pattern, the same animal, stuffed it and wrapped each special gift with love.

Remembering your labor always brings bittersweet tears to my eyes. I can see you sewing, tearing out seams, redoing stitches, winding bobbins, cutting with pinking shears, embroidering names, and stuffing animals--all the while humming along with Christmas carols by Andy Williams and Bing Crosby playing on the stereo. The records were worn and scratched; we could anticipate each time someone would need to get up and manually move the needle on the vinyl LP to stop the repeating of "sounding joy."

As lovely as that all sounds, there was always a sense of anxiety hovering like an impending storm on those same December evenings because of Dad. You always did your best to shelter us from the storm when he came home drunk. He often "stormed" on holidays. You made Christmas special, but I have to admit, to this day I still feel anxious around Christmas and set expectations too high. I think I'm always striving to create the kind of Christmas that Bing and you were always dreaming of. But the reality is that even Norman Rockwell families probably have their moments, right? Those red-haired kids with freckles were probably teased unmercifully at school and terrified of spilling gravy down the front of their smocked dresses and sweater vests. No family is that perfect, right? Tell that to the *Saturday Evening Post*.

There is no script for everyone to follow to ensure peace. Thank the Lord, there is Scripture that gives you the best chance at having lasting peace. Thanks for always keeping Christ in Christmas, Mom.

MOM, when your big heart failed in June 1999, we found fifty blankets folded neatly on your bedroom dresser. You and your team of knitters made them for Project Linus. This non-profit was a perfect fit for your talent and heart. We were not surprised when you started your own chapter in Pueblo as an octogenarian.

What an example of dedication you were as you drove all over town delivering the hand-made gifts of comfort to children in hospitals or oncology centers. The kids cuddled up in their "made with love" blankets as they endured the slow drip, drip, drip of chemotherapy. You kept a well-organized file of index cards arranged by donor. You had a card for each donor, listing their name, how many blankets they made, and the dates you received the blankets. You inspired woman all over the state to contribute blankets. We were so proud of the article in the Pueblo newspaper thanking you for your "saintly work in comforting ill children."

After you went to heaven, I also found the Project Linus thank you notes you sent to each one of your contributors. I keep that old tin file box on a shelf of my bookcase. I love to look at your unique back-slanting handwriting on the cards and envision the joyful look you probably had on your face as you made each new entry. There was also a little note you wrote at the very bottom of the file box:

"I believe that when we do what we love to do, we touch other people in ways unknown to us. I have been very grateful to know I have touched a child's life in the process of having such a great time myself."

At eighty-seven, you regularly delivered knitted blankets to over a half a dozen locations all over town. We learned at your funeral from the director of the Linus Project that you had made and delivered over three hundred blankets by yourself. No wonder the Linus Project dedicated their ten thousandth blanket to you! You so deserved that Blanketeer of the Year Award.

I'm so proud of you, Mom. What a way to honor your own grandson (Jason) following his own successful battle against cancer the year prior to your Project Linus involvement.

BUT, Mom, the absolute greatest gift you gave me was making Jesus real to us, like a member of our family. I now know He was the one who made us a member of His family not the other way around. His picture was the first one in the photo section of your wallet, followed by the rest of your kids, grandkids, and pets.

The over-sized picture of Jesus with his arms stretched wide open, which hung at the top of the stairs , brought me comfort and reminded me of His unfailing and trustworthy protection. Since this picture was on the wall just outside my bedroom door, I told Him good night before going to bed every night. Did you know I did that? Or was that your plan when you hung it there?

THANK you for being my mentor and inspiration for the past couple of days with Ruby. Though it required a little shove— from Jesus—you taught me to know better than to leave a woman and her dog sitting by a curb in the cold.

Thanks for the memories, Mom. I miss you.

SEVEN

Hello It's Me

---

*S*ix days after I got home, I called the motel to check manager of the mom-and-pop motel. He said Ruby had checked out early that morning, and the last they'd seen her, she was hitchhiking with her dog.

I hung up the phone feeling upset. Ruby still had one more day at the motel! *Why in the world had she checked out early?* I thought. I doubted she had many true friends she could rely on.

I was frantic to help, but there was nothing I could do.

The next morning, my phone rang.

"Hello, it's me, Ruby."

"Thank goodness you called!" I said with great relief. "I've been so worried about you!"

"Well, I didn't think I should call and bother you again after you done so much for me already, but this here lady I'm stayin' with said you wouldn't have given me your information if it wasn't ok for me to use it. She took me in, but it's hard on her to have another person to feed. Here you talk to her."

"Hello, Cy. Ruby just handed me the phone, so I guess she

wants us to talk." The woman chuckled. She sounded nice. "My name is Dee."

As it turned out, Jesus brought a friend to Ruby. The night after Ruby had left the motel, Dee had found her at a park, lying on her blanket with Lizzie Lou. This Good Samaritan invited Ruby home to her trailer and let Ruby and Lizzie Lou spend the night on her couch. When Dee asked Ruby the following morning if she had any friends she could call, Ruby showed her the piece of paper with my name and phone number.

"Dee, thank you so much for telling Ruby to call me and more than that thank you for being kind enough to bring her home for the night," I said. "I've been so worried."

"I was glad to. I work at a truck stop café where she'd visited with her little dog once or twice. Yesterday when she came in, I asked her where she was staying. She told me she'd been put up in a motel by a friend, but now she was going to sleep in the park. Of course, that worried me, so when I got off work I went by the park and found her just where she said she'd be. I invited her to come home with me for the night. Believe me, it took some convincing, but then she agreed. She told me 'Angels seem to be comin' outta nowhere lately.'"

"Ruby is very independent, so I can relate to the amount of convincing it took to get her to your place. She doesn't trust easily. Good job!"

"I heard Ruby tell you it was hard on me to have her stay," she said. "It's difficult because I'm in a mobile home park that doesn't allow dogs, and it is a very small place. Also, I work nights and some days. It's just not easy to adjust to an extra person with my hours and my limited income."

"Dee, Ruby and I totally understand," I assured her. "We

are just so grateful for your kindness and willingness to bring her home with you."

"Ruby told me you are a Christian, Cy. It made me so happy to know she met someone who would show her the love of Jesus. I am also very committed to my faith," Dee explained. "I have this afternoon off, and if it is alright with you, I can bring Ruby part of the way to Denver. We can meet at a gas station about halfway between Buena Vista and Denver."

"That would be fine. May I speak with Ruby for a second?"

"Hi, Cy," Ruby said tentatively. "Sounds like some plans are being cooked up, and I ain't sure you want me back. I promise it ain't goin' to be for long. I need to get me my own place."

"I'm so relieved to hear you aren't sleeping at a truck stop or park bench, Ruby. Of course I want you to come home with me until we can find you a place to live," I said as convincingly as I could.

On the drive to meet Dee and Ruby, I had a heart-to-heart talk with Jesus. I knew He already knew what I was feeling, but I needed to say it out loud to Him:

"Dear Jesus, I am feeling very overwhelmed right now. In fact, if I'm being totally honest, I feel taken advantage of. Not by Ruby, but by You, Lord. I will be forever changed by meeting Ruby and being able to show her what You look like in the flesh. It was an honor to be used to reveal your Holy Spirit to Ruby. Thank you for choosing me and trusting me. But once again, I have to ask You, 'Am I prepared for this?' "

I thought a moment before adding, "And it's not just me. Is my *family* prepared for Ruby to come home and live with us for an undetermined amount of time? Is it fair to them? Bruce has the biggest heart on the planet, but now I'm asking him to go to Mars. Whitney enjoyed being with Ruby and Lizzie Lou, but will an extended stay make what originally felt like a good deed begin to feel like an unfair burden? Lord, am I prepared to take on the responsibility of finding a home for a woman I've only known for a week? You know me better than anyone. I can't even balance a checkbook. How can I bring balance to someone's life?"

"Are you finished, Cy?"

"No, not even close. I am very busy. I have my volunteer work. I'm in a Bible Study. You wouldn't want me to fall behind on those lessons, would You? I drive Whitney to all of her practices and games. I help out with the athletic teams. I am the snack and party mom. Plus, Ryan is still in law school."

I felt a check in my spirit.

"Okay, God, I'll admit Ryan isn't a good excuse since I don't need to drive him anywhere or plan parties or snacks. But there's also Bruce. He really likes to have his quiet time after work, and Lizzie Lou will make sure that doesn't happen. Plus, Bruce, Whitney, and I go out to dinner several times a week (to give our stomachs a rest from my cooking), and Ruby doesn't like to go out (although my cooking might change her mind). Anyway, God, you know what I am trying to say. Having Ruby as a guest for an extended period of time won't be convenient."

"Convenient? Cy, are you hearing yourself?" From what I could tell, God didn't sound at all impressed with my laundry list of concerns. *"I'm not concerned about your falling behind on your Bible studies, I am more concerned on your falling behind on living what you've studied. If you recall, I asked Moses to lead my people out of Egypt. He told Me he could not lead because he lacked speaking skills. I gave him a great spokesperson in Aaron. In other words, I'm pretty great at equipping folks for what I ask them to do. Besides, if you think it's inconvenient to actually live out what you're learning, to do the things I'm calling you to do, think about the inconvenience of* not *walking the walk. I doubt Moses thought*

forty years wandering in the dessert was convenient. And Jonah would tell you that living for three days in the belly of a whale wasn't convenient either."

"Desert? Fish? God, now you're scaring me. I'm like a hothouse flower. I need a little coddling. I'm like the princess who can't sleep on a pea. And like Goldilocks, I need things just right."

"I'm at your door, Cy. I'm knocking. Will you open this door and let me reveal my holy plan for you and for Ruby? I won't enter where I am not welcome. Will you push the door open and let me in?"

It seemed shove had come to push.

"I'll try to be worthy of Your trust, Lord—and Ruby's trust, too."

WE MET AT A GAS STATION. Dee was a lovely woman, and after we loaded Ruby's things back in the car, we hugged and shared our gratefulness for each other's concern for our new friend. Ruby thanked Dee for "taking her in."

Ruby and her scraggly sidekick took their places in my car.

"Buckle up, Ruby," I reminded her as usual.

During our drive back to Denver, I asked Ruby what had happened to all of her Buena Vista friends, and why she headed back to the park where Dee found her. She wasn't very forthcoming on that topic, but she did have some other interesting revelations to share.

"I'm diabetic, type 2. Ain't been on my medications for quite a while," she confessed. In fact, she hadn't been on her medications for well over two weeks, ever since she'd been in a hospital in Colorado Springs, not long before she met me. She explained that she had ended up in the hospital 'cause she had to have a toe amputated due to bad circulation and blocked arteries. Hence the one slipper and one shoe.

"Ruby, I don't understand. How have you been living without your medicine?" I was astounded.

"Oh, I got disability and Medicaid," she said nonchalantly. "Now I'm set for a while 'cause after visitin' my brother I got me my disability check at the post office in Buena Vista. I thumbed my way over there on Monday, and it was waitin' for me. I just ain't got no doctor right now."

"Why does the government send your checks to Buena Vista?" I asked, once again having trouble tracking with her story.

"I'd been livin' in a trailer up there, but it started smellin' like gas. And that old boy who owned the trailer said he didn't smell nothin' and wasn't gonna fix it. So, I packed up and left before the thing blew up on me."

"So you actually lived in Buena Vista?" I kept trying to unweave the web.

"Yeah, I wanted to be near my brother after I left that mean old boy I was married to," she answered.

"Okay, now I'm confused. You were recently married? I thought that was a long time ago."

"Well it was a few years back. I told you about him. I stored my stuff in a storage yard in Commerce City and been payin' on it until I could get me a place."

She always revealed these bits of information as though they shouldn't be news to me. It felt as though she had dumped three thousand puzzle pieces on a card table and it was up to me to put the picture together.

"Where had you been living when I met you?" I kept probing.

"Mostly parks and truck stops since I left Buena Vista. I was at a truck stop in Commerce City the night before I hitched my way to that church where you found me. I'd been checkin' to make sure the storage place still had my things. Course I'd been in the hospital in Colorado Springs right before that."

Of course.

Maybe *puzzle* wasn't the right word. It felt more like I'd been handed a mystery to solve. Maybe I needed a giant blank wall like you see on detective shows where I could tape sticky notes and photos along with newspaper clippings to make some sort of time line of Ruby's life. As it was, all I could do was listen and hope my brain didn't explode.

A FEW DAYS after coming back to our house, Ruby got very anxious and was ready to move on. But to where?

To add to the three-ring circus in our home, my older brother moved in with us for a while. During their combined visit, Greg and Ruby became smoking buddies on our back patio. Lizzie Lou seemed to enjoy these smoking soirees, and she never barked at Greg. They were quite the threesome, sitting out on our back porch at night, huddled in coats sharing an empty soup can as an ashtray.

I run a first-class operation.

One afternoon after we'd watched Oprah and Dr. Phil (and before *Wheel of Fortune* came on), it seemed like a good time to broach the topic of Ruby's future plans and housing options.

"So Ruby, you said you have a lot of things in a storage unit. Where did they come from? Did you have them in a house or apartment at some time? How did you afford the payments or rent?" I pried as gently as possible. My biggest fear was to make her feel unwelcome.

"Ya know, I got me a Section 8 Housing voucher," she said

casually as she got up from the couch and headed toward the sliding glass doors off the kitchen that led to the smoking area.

I had no idea what that was but had to wait until the smoke cleared and Ruby came back inside to ask her what a Section 8 Housing voucher was. She told me it allowed her to rent a place at a much lower rate.

Although our previous "voucher" experience didn't exactly pan out, this Section 8 thing seemed like an idea worth pursuing.

EIGHT

Ain't No Elevator High Enough

---

*T*he next morning, Ruby, Lizzie Lou, and I ventured out to follow up on the Section 8 voucher. I had called Adams County Human Services and received a recorded message with their address and hours.

I was totally unfamiliar with this area of town. This was pre-GPS, and we accidentally left the directions I printed from my computer on the kitchen counter. Ruby was certain she could lead me right to the place. I have to admit she did get us pretty close.

After a few errant turns (several being my fault), we arrived at our destination. We let Lizzie Lou out of the car for a minute while Ruby smoked the remainder of a previously stubbed-out cigarette.

"Okay, Ruby," I said as she finished the cigarette. "Let's go find you a place to live."

Three steps into the building, and I received a news flash.

Ruby announced, "I can't ride in that elevator."

"Why not?"

"I'm scared of elevators. Last time I was here a lady had to hold my hand all the way up to the fourth floor. Then I couldn't get out."

"So, what happened? Did you ever make it out?" I asked.

"Of course I did, but it took me three tries. I kept openin' the elevator door before it could start goin' up. Finally, the lady blocked me from pushin' them door buttons, and when we got to the fourth floor, she walked me out to the line in the hall. The line was so long I never did get to talk to anybody. I done that every day for almost a week and never got to the front of the line. So I ain't goin' up that elevator today unless I'm sure they'll see me," she declared adamantly.

Every day for a week? I was amazed she'd found that many people to hold her hand during all those elevator rides. *Well,* I reasoned, *she does have a way about her.*

I patted her shoulder. "Well, I'm with you today. I'll hold your hand, and I promise we will get to the front of the line sometime today or else!"

This struck her as funny, and she giggled as I gently pushed her into the elevator. She kept her eyes closed, I held her hand, and in less than twenty seconds we were at our floor. She wasn't kidding about the line. There were at least thirty people standing in the hallway.

"See, I told you. There ain't no way we are gonna get to the front today."

"Are you sure we are in the right place? I mean we certainly aren't going to wait in this line all day just to find out we are supposed to be somewhere else. Wait here and save our place. I'm just going to go check." I must have said it with some authority because for once she didn't talk back.

I began to serpentine my way through the queue of people. "Excuse me, I'm not cutting line. I just need to ask a question. I'll be really quick. I promise." I said this repeatedly as I made my way toward the counter. As I look back, it kind of felt like the parting of the Red Sea. I just kept moving forward and the line just kept parting.

I finally reached my destination. "Excuse me, ma'am," I said, trying to get the attention of a weary-looking window warden. She kept her head down but looked up at me with her eyes peeking over her tortoise framed reading glasses perched on her nose.

I didn't let it deter me from my mission.

"I just have a quick question," I explained. "Am I in the right place?"

She just stared at me.

"Oh, sorry," I said cheerfully. "You have no idea of the place I want to be, do you?"

"No. Why don't you enlighten me?" She said with some attitude.

"I'm with my friend, and she is in need of housing. She has been here before, but never made it to this window, so I don't even know if this is the right place," I said as quickly as possible. "Anyway, she says she has something called a Section 8 Voucher. Does that ring any bells with you?"

Take a breath, Cy, I told myself.

"Why isn't your friend here?"

"Oh, she is. I just didn't want her to stand in line or walk any farther than she needed to. She is missing her big toe."

"Okay, well, I'm sorry to hear that," the woman said, and she sounded sincere. "You say she has a Section 8 Housing Voucher and has been here before? What's her full name, date of birth, and current residence?" Now she seemed a little more engaged.

"Her name is Ruby Jean, but I'm not sure of her birthdate.

It's something 1945, I think. That's just it, she has no residence. I found her a couple of weeks ago."

"You found her?" The clerk pursed her brows. "What do you mean you *found* her?

Another woman with her back to us was doing some filing behind the window warden, and she turned around to get a look at who was telling this tale.

"I guess, I met her, would be a better choice of words. She is my friend now and not someone I found by the side of the road. She has been staying with my family and now she really needs a place of her own. My brother is staying with us, too—"

Once again, I had to remind myself to breathe.

"—and her dog is driving my husband nuts. Okay, fine, actually her dog is driving *me* nuts. So, am I in the right place to find her a place to live?"

Suddenly the lady who had been filing in the background stepped up to the window and spoke. "Why don't you go get Ruby and bring her here, and we can get some more information?"

"Okay, but I cut in front of all these people and I don't want to be unfair." I confessed loud enough for those near the front of the line to hear. I wanted them to know I was remorseful and not rude.

"These people are all waiting to *apply* for a Section 8 voucher. It sounds like Ruby already has one. I'm Mrs. Garcia, and Ruby would fall into the area I serve. Please go get her, and we can talk in my office."

"Thank you, that would be great! I'll be right back with her." I was so excited; it felt like I had "taken one small leap for mankind."

The sea parted again. Apparently those closest to the window had overheard the whole conversation and wanted to see where this thing was going. They practically escorted me to get Ruby.

"Ruby, come on," I called out. We get to talk to someone. We get to go to the front of the line!"

Ruby grabbed her cane and eased herself up from the bench to follow me back through the line.

Once again, I apologized to total strangers as I jostled past them. "Excuse us. Thank you. Last time, I promise."

Mrs. Garcia was holding the door open that led to her private office when we approached.

She was very kind to Ruby and apologized that she had visited the office so many times without being helped. She got all of Ruby's necessary information, and Ruby reached in her duffel bag and pulled out the Section 8 voucher, which was actually still valid.

"It all seems in order, Ruby. I'm glad you have a friend to help you."

"She ain't just a friend; she's an angel. I ain't even kiddin,' " Ruby explained. "She took me home with her. Oprah never took no stranger home with her."

I rolled my eyes hoping to convey to Mrs. Garcia that I wanted no part of this celestial title.

"Well," said Mrs. Garcia, "you and your angel need to go out front again and start looking through the books listing Adams County apartment rentals with Section 8 designations. Then, you need to start calling and checking on availability."

This sounded far more hopeful than it looked once we got out in the waiting area where the rental books were stacked in a corner like booster chairs. They were as big as phone books. Some were current, some were a month or two old, and most had pages torn out of them. Ruby and I sat down with the books on our laps and felt overwhelmed.

"How does anyone know where to start?" I lamented. I don't even know this part of town and she needed to stay in the same county in which the voucher was granted—I was also unfamiliar with it. Several of the housing clients sympathized with me and agreed that it was a hopeless task. It would, no doubt, take weeks to find a place.

A lady leaning against the wall offered a suggestion. "You should check over at Greenview Terrace. I heard they might have vacant apartments, and I know my sister lives there on a Section 8. It's a pretty nice place; they keep it up pretty good."

"Oh, my gosh, thank you. That is so nice of you. Do you know the number or address or anything?"

"I've got it right here, hang on." The lady behind the window offered. She was practically leaping out of her desk chair to retrieve the information.

"Here you go. Here's the number of the Greenwood Terrace Apartments." She handed Ruby the slip of paper through her sliding window.

I opened my cell phone, called the number, and spoke to the manager. She informed me a one bedroom on the ground floor had just become vacant that morning. They allowed small dogs. (I would never tell Lizzie Lou that she fit the "small" size criteria. It would destroy her.) With Ruby's voucher, the apartment was a fraction of what it normally would have cost. Her monthly disability would cover the rent and hopefully leave enough money for food and utilities.

Mrs. Garcia emerged from her office to give us another bit of news. "The apartment will need to have a Section 8 inspector come to make sure it meets their standards. It will also need a fresh coat of pain. I'm guessing Ruby will be able to move there in about ten days."

"Ruby, why don't you go grab a quick smoke while I talk to

Mrs. Garcia for a few more minutes. I'll ride down in the elevator with you."

"You feelin' alright, Cy?" Ruby said with a grin. "You ain't never told me to go smoke before!"

"I must have a fever."

Now, this is where Jesus began showing off big time.

I went back to ask Mrs. Garcia if there was any way Ruby could get in the apartment sooner. Mrs. Garcia explained that most of the delay would be arranging for an inspector to schedule a visit to the apartment. That usually takes about a week or longer.

Seeing the look on my face, she excused herself and made a phone call.

When she returned, she said, "I can't believe it! The inspector I called had a cancellation and can go to the apartment tomorrow! After that, I called the apartment manager and she had already written a work order to get the apartment painted in the next day or two."

Mrs. Garcia was so moved by Ruby's and my new friendship she was eager to be a part of a solution. Apparently, the inspector and the property manager wanted to jump on board the Ruby train also. The property manager even had a nice couch and chair she would give to Ruby if she would like to have it.

The apartment manager called me back to let me know Ruby would need a first and last month's rent deposit and a $500 deposit for Lizzie Lou.

Seriously, what person in need of government housing has that kind of money?

I called my banker.

"Hello, honey, guess what?"

"Lucy, is that you?"

"Yes, Ricky."

Bruce said he would pay the expenses to enable Ruby to get in the apartment.

When I hung up with Bruce, I hugged Mrs. Garcia and the clerk at the window, too. Next, I hugged the lady who told us about the apartment and high-fived a few others in line who seemed genuinely happy that Ruby had successfully navigated this hopeless process of finding shelter. They felt her pain *and* her joy. Ruby seemed to give them hope.

When I got down to the parking lot, Ruby was on her second or third cigarette. She was like a kid who had just been given permission to spend fifteen minutes in a candy store unattended. She didn't look like a kid, though. She looked very tired. When I told her the news about the apartment, she began to shake her head in weary disbelief. I reached for her hand and bowed my head to thank Jesus for His help. Ruby bowed her head too and said, "Thank you, Jesus."

On the drive home she told me nobody had ever treated her as nice as when she was with me. She said it was because I had status. I winced at that word. She again referred to herself as a bum that people didn't give any respect to when she was on her own. She reminded me she'd been at that housing office every day for over a week before she met me. "I ain't never made it to the front of the line before closing."

"You say *status*. I say *Jesus*."

Later it became an inside joke. When we ventured out we wondered whether I should wear my "status clothes and attitude" in case we were going to be waiting in any lines. I also warned Ruby I never wanted to hear her call herself a bum again. "God doesn't make bums. He makes super women like us!"

Friends and family members who knew about Ruby were eager to gather furniture and kitchen items for her new apartment. My nephew had a truck and helped us unload her storage unit. There wasn't much in the way of furniture or household goods, but there were boxes and boxes of miscellaneous papers and artwork her brother made for her in prison. Although I understood how she treasured her brother's artwork, I wondered how she could justify paying to store all that stuff. Then it dawned on me. It was her stuff, and she valued it. I also have a storage unit. It's called my house, and you never saw so much stuff.

After a long day of setting up her furniture and putting away her kitchen items, Bruce, Whitney, and I left Ruby Jean sitting on her brocade floral couch with Lizzie Lou on her lap and Mario Brothers jumping around on the TV screen. Ruby had gotten very good at "Intendo," so Whitney gave Ruby her Nintendo. It was the best housewarming gift ever!

Ruby wasn't homeless anymore.

NINE

All Is Not Well

*R*uby had an address at last.

Originally, I thought she had only one missing toe, which had been amputated due to her diabetes. It turned out her other foot had a middle toe missing for the same reason. The boxes of pills we'd retrieved from her storage unit were alarming. Why did she have all these prescriptions? What were they for? How was she doing without them all this time? Certainly, her diabetes wasn't being managed at all. The next important item on the agenda became finding her a primary care doctor.

Within a few days, she located a general physician who took Medicaid. His office was not too far from her apartment. She took a cab to see him. I was proud of her for taking the initiative to find a doctor and was relieved knowing she would get back on her diabetes medications and get a checkup.

Before her second appointment, she asked if I could take her and meet the doctor. She wanted to make sure I liked him.

She made the appointment for 8:00 a.m. I lived about thirty miles south of Ruby, which meant my rush hour drive time would be at least an hour or more. I must have forgotten to share that with her that I'm also not a morning person.

When I arrived at her apartment, she was already sitting out front on a cement ledge smoking a freshly rolled cigarette.

"I thought you was going to forget me," she complained. She sounded truly worried.

"Ruby, I wouldn't forget you. Besides it's only 7:30. Why are you out here in the cold? I would have come to the door to get you."

"I didn't want to miss my appointment, and like I said, I thought you mighta got busy and forgot me. So, I was gonna wait a few more minutes and then see if I could hitch a ride."

Clearly, she still didn't totally trust me to follow through with what I told her I would do, even though I had a stellar record for being exactly where I said I would be—and on time. Her doubting made me sad and a little bit mad. Thankfully, God gave me the grace to remember she had a fifty-four-year history of people letting her down, not showing up, not caring.

Ruby's trust would take more than a few months to earn.

She finished her cigarette, picked up her cane and huge leather handbag. It was ornately tooled with strands of leather fringe hanging from the zipper. I told her it was beautiful, and she proudly told me her brother made it for her in prison. It had been with her things in storage. When we got to her car door, I volunteered to hold her handbag, so she could maneuver her way into the low passenger seat of my car. She handed it to me, and it almost pulled my shoulder out of place.

"This purse has to weigh thirty pounds, Ruby! How can you carry this thing? What in the heck is in here?"

"I got my papers, my money, my pills is all. I can't leave things in my apartment; they might get stolen."

"Seriously, that stuff couldn't weigh this much. Do you bowl? Do you have a bowling ball in there?" I joked.

"Nah, I bowled once or twice a long time ago but never had my own ball. Could be the quarters."

"The quarters?"

We were starting to sound like a Seinfeld episode.

"For the washing machines at the apartment. I walked down to a nearby bank to cash my disability check and got me $50 in quarters. I like to keep my clothes clean."

I started the car and began to pull away from the curb.

"Right, well I guess we better head to the doctor, we can have him look at your shoulder while we are there. It has to be dislocated from the weight of that handbag."

"You're funny."

"That's what I keep telling you! Now, what's the doctor's address?"

"I ain't got his address with me. I left it on the kitchen counter." This was starting to become a habit.

"Shall we go back and get it?" I asked.

"Nah, I know the way. Besides we'd be late if we went back, and it would upset Lizzie Lou."

Serenity now.

"Okay," I relented. "Just tell me where to turn."

"Go straight on down this street for a few blocks and turn right, where the Wendy's is on the corner."

I have to say, those were my kind of instructions. I am not big on street names or north, south, east, or west directions either.

"Okay, I turned right. Now where?"

"Go straight about four more blocks until you get to a sign that says there's a dip in the road. Then go two more blocks past the shopping center on the right and turn right. There's a

Mexican food place in that shopping center. Wonder if it's any good? I can make some of the best Mexican food you ever had. I like it plenty hot. When I get—turn left!"

"When?"

"Now!"

"You are going to be the death of us Ruby Jean!" I laughed as we careened around the corner on screeching tires.

"Just keep goin'. There it is; that grey house on the left with the ramp."

I parked in the lot on the side of the office, unloaded Ruby, her handbag, and cane.

"Ruby, it's pretty impressive that you found your way back to this office after only being here once before," I said with admiration.

"I got me a knack with my bearings. I watch for things on the road I can remember. I've always been good about knowin' my way around. It's important to know where you're goin' when you hitch a ride."

Makes sense, I thought.

"Good morning, Ruby." the receptionist greeted her warmly.

"Mornin', this here's my friend, Cy." Ruby introduced me like I was about to perform.

"Nice to meet you. Go ahead and have a seat. The doctor's running a little behind. Oh, before you sit down, Ruby Jean, I'll need your Medicaid card and your two-dollar copay."

Ruby handed over the two dollars and the Medicaid card. She waited for her receipt and card. She also asked why she had to pay another two dollars since she had just been there a week ago.

I took a seat next to two coughing patients and across from

four others with less conspicuous maladies. There was one chair remaining for Ruby in sick bay.

How could the doctor be running late already? I mused. *It's only 8:00 a.m. for cryin' out loud!* There were already six people before us. I looked around for a magazine rack, thinking they might have Oprah's magazine.

An hour later a nurse emerged from a side door. Holding a clipboard, she called out "Ruby?"

I had just witnessed yet another one of Ruby's admirable qualities: she was patient. While I was getting more aggravated by the minute during the long wait, Ruby had calmly settled into it. But then, she was used to waiting.

"That's me! Come on, Cy let's go."

"Are you sure you want me in the room with you? I don't want to invade your privacy," I explained. I was feeling a little reluctant. I am not inclined to let anyone in the doctor's office with me. I can barely tolerate the doctor.

"Yeah, I told the Doc I was bringing you, and he said he wanted to meet you. Besides, like I told you, I wanted you to see if you thought he was any good."

How could I argue with that? We walked together with the nurse down a hallway.

"Good to see you again, Ruby," the nurse said pleasantly. "Now let's have you get on the scale. Then I'll get you in a room. The doctor won't be too much longer."

"Hand me your purse, Ruby," I suggested. "You don't want to have it on the scale with you."

"This here is my friend, Cy," Ruby explained to the nurse as she handed me her bowling ball carrier. "The one I was telling you about."

"Oh, yes, hello," the nurse greeted me, then said to Ruby, "I thought you said her name was Angel." She smiled at me. "I'm Kathleen."

Kathleen wrote something down on her clipboard. "Okay, Ruby, five two and 182 pounds, same as last week. Let me get you in a room and the doctor will be with you shortly."

Ruby used the step stool to climb onto the exam table. I took a seat on the short round stool with wheels. I started pedaling with my feet and rolling around the little office. When I bumped into the plastic skeleton standing in the corner, Ruby scolded me like an exasperated mom. "Cy, get off that stool! It's the doctor's. Sit in that chair by the door."

I had just made it to the chair before the doctor came in.

"Hi, Doctor," Ruby greeted him. "This here is my friend, Cy."

I said I was glad to meet him and thanked him for taking care of Ruby.

"Of course, Ruby's told me all about how you found her."

"It was a good find," I said. We both grinned.

After some friendly banter with Ruby and questions about how she was feeling, the doctor took her blood pressure and listened to her chest.

"Cy, I don't know if Ruby has told you, but she has some serious health concerns. I started her on some medications for her diabetes last week. We will need to run some blood tests and check on her arteries and circulation. She also needs to make some very big changes to her diet, and stop smoking! I will make arrangements for the tests and have my nurse call her. Ruby, do you have a way to get to these appointments?" He asked while scribbling on his chart.

"I can get me a cab, but it costs a lot of money."

"Cy, do you live nearby?" the doctor inquired.

"Actually, I live about an hour away, but I can get her to any appointments," I heard myself say. Honestly, my lips were moving, but Jesus was doing the talking.

"Well, that's helpful, but have you looked into getting a motorized scooter? I am pretty sure Medicaid would cover all or most of the cost. I can give you a prescription and letter explaining her medical situation to make sure she qualifies."

"That would be great, we will look into it right away. I know it would help her to be able to get around a little better."

"I told you, he was a nice man for a doctor," Ruby proclaimed right in front of him.

"Thanks, for that kind endorsement, Ruby," the doctor said, laughing. "Cy, it was a pleasure meeting you. I will write up the prescriptions, so have a seat in the waiting room for a minute. Ruby, remember no more smoking or chocolate. I'll see you in about four weeks."

Ruby wanted to "have a quick puff" before we even got in the car.

"Are you kidding? What did the doctor just say to you?" I was a bit perturbed.

"He said not to have a cigarette with chocolate," she said, and her smile told me she knew better.

"No! That's my final answer." I scolded her like a three-year-old. I halfway expected her to say, "You're not the boss of me!"

TEN

She's on a Roll

"*W*hat are you looking for in a scooter?" the lonely salesman inquired.

Ruby and I were just walking in the door when we were accosted by a man in a plaid sport coat that reminded me of a seventies leisure suit.

"I need me one with wheels," Ruby said.

Ruby's lack of filter never ceased to crack me up.

Unfazed, he took us to what appeared to be the bare-bones model in motorized scooters.

"Actually, we need to look at something a little sturdier and more comfortable," I interjected. "Medicaid likely will be paying for it. We have a prescription from her doctor."

"In that case, we have a number of models that should meet your qualifications." He visibly perked up and started reeling off model numbers that included XLTs and deluxe, and I think I even remember hearing the word *brougham*.

Just as we were almost glassy-eyed from plaid and hyperbole, we had a *Christmas Vacation* Christmas tree moment. An almost halo-like glow fell over a bright red scooter in the back of the showroom. I was shocked there wasn't a velvet rope surrounding it.

"That one," I said, pointing," what about that one?"

"You've got good taste. That's the XXXLT SUPERDELUXE 10,000 Brougham," he said, or something like that.

"Ruby, sit on this one." I nudged her forward.

"I like that red color and the basket. It'll hold my groceries."

"Can we take it for a spin around the block?" I had my doubts but had to ask.

"Uh, no, but you can drive it around the showroom."

Ruby tossed her handbag in the front basket and slowly got in the seat. A big smile lit up her face, and it actually did feel like Christmas.

"This is sure comfortable, but it's probably too high for Medicaid to cover."

"I can handle the paperwork, file the claim, and have it delivered to you by the end of the week," said the man in plaid.

True to his word, Ruby was driving her bright red scooter on Friday.

Thank you, Lord! I said to him the first time I saw her on her scooter. *A bright ruby red scooter. You are always in the details.*

WITH RUBY'S newfound freedom came a different problem. How would she call for help if she needed it? She had already called for an ambulance twice. She had a landline in her apartment so her brother could call her collect from prison. That meant that as long as she was in her apartment, she could always get in touch with someone if she needed help. But now that she was riding around outside of the apartment on her scooter, I knew I would feel more comfortable if she had a cell phone. So we added Ruby to our AT&T Family Plan. I think

Bruce bought the cell phone as much for me as for Ruby. He got tired of me pacing and imagining every dangerous situation Ruby might encounter on the street. He often reminded me that she had survived many years without our help. I understood this, but now she was our friend. That changed everything.

Winter didn't deter Ruby. She had no qualms about plowing through the snow on her new vehicle. Her favorite activity right after her Social Security check came was to browse ARC, which is a Colorado-based nonprofit thrift store that sells donated clothing and housing goods at great prices. She called it Arch. I didn't bother correcting her as her quirky mispronunciations—like still calling Nintendo "Intendo"—were endearing to me.

I accompanied her to "Arch" one day after we'd been running a few errands that weren't scooter friendly. I became a believer. They had some fabulous bargains. We found a long winter coat for her. It was the puffy kind that makes you look like the Michelin Man. Because of her short stature, she was truly covered from head to toe. A scarf, mittens, and a hat completed the ensemble. She let me buy the twenty-dollar coat after much protesting. She would not allow me to pay for the scarf, mittens, and hat. This was part of the lesson God was trying to teach me. Ruby had pride; she didn't want to take advantage of our financial differences. She proudly made her purchase and bought Whitney a necklace for two dollars.

When I got home that day, I found a little angel pin hidden in my purse. She found a far less thoughtful, or sacrificial, fifty-dollar bill hidden in hers.

I'll be the first to admit that the first few months of our relationship had been spent in a crisis management mode. But as each crisis was resolved, I began to see Ruby in a changed light. I saw the woman she might have been if her circumstances had been different. For one thing, her appearance began to alter significantly. Her trips to Arch revealed her penchant for bright-colored outfits and matching accessories.

I picked her up for lunch one day. Lizzie Lou barked like I might be an ax murderer. Ruby yelled, "Hush up! You stop it Lizzie Lou! It's Cy!" while fumbling with the dead bolt and chain lock on her door. She opened the door leaving the chain barricade until she was certain it was actually me on the other side. She shut the door to release the chain and then reopened it to let me in. Lizzie Lou continued barking maniacally for a few more minutes. Finally, when the commotion died down, I stepped back and took a good look at Ruby. Who was this woman?

"Ruby, I love your outfit. Is it new?"

"I got it for four dollars over at Arch." She smiled with pride.

"That color is great on you. I could never pull off purple, but you are rockin' it!"

"It's my favorite color. Always has been since I was a little girl," she shared.

Upon further inspection I noticed she wore pink nail polish and a pink and purple ribbon around the bun of hair on top of her head. She had a little dash of blush on her cheeks and purple butterfly earrings. She looked beautiful.

We had no agenda that day—no appointments, no problems to fix. It was a girls' day out, a day for fun. I was the one who felt underdressed this time, and I couldn't have been happier.

"Where should we go for lunch?" I asked.

"I ain't had Mexican food in a long time." (Really? It seemed like yesterday to me.) "It's my favorite. I can really make some great green chili. I'm gonna come over and make you and your husband a big batch one of these days," she declared proudly.

Before long, we were seated with a basket of chips between us, enjoying what was becoming a regular tradition. I gulped ice water with my very spicy burrito while she poured hot sauce all over hers. We laughed and joked. For the first time I didn't feel like a rescuer. I felt like a girlfriend.

ELEVEN

Enlarging My Territory

---

*E*very other Tuesday I made the trip to Ruby's. We began calling these our Ruby Tuesdays.

One Tuesday we were in the car driving to Arch after going to a Mexican restaurant for lunch when Ruby said she wanted to talk to me about something.

She told me her brother had called her the night before with some news. He was up for parole. He had never been up for parole before and told Ruby that one person would be able to speak to the board on his behalf. He asked Ruby if she would do it.

"I ain't no good talking to them parole people. I just get mad. I'm sure to start cussin' them out," Ruby admitted before getting to her real request. She wanted me to be the one person allowed to speak in defense of her brother at his upcoming parole hearing.

"But Ruby, I've never even met your brother. I know how much you love him, but I've only spoken to him on the phone. I don't think I'm the right person."

In the end, she convinced me, and I agreed.

Ruby's brother (I'll call him Sam) had already served nineteen years in maximum security in Canyon City and Sterling, Colorado. Due to good behavior, he was currently serving his time in Buena Vista, a minimum-security facility. Ruby had served the same number of years in her own prison of helplessness, heartache, and grieving over her brother. The longer I knew her, the more touched I was by her abiding love for her younger brother. Her loyalty certainty never wavered. She was positive he did not commit the crime for which he was imprisoned.

The parole board hearing was in a few weeks. I made plans to attend with Ruby and filled out all the paper work and sent them a photocopy of my driver's license so I could get my name on the approved visitors list at the prison.

While waiting for the parole date, I wrote letters to the Warden and every parole board member, begging them to consider parole for Ruby's brother. I anguished over each line, hoping my plea for compassion and the promise that Bruce and I would help him would make a difference.

I also spoke with Sam's case manager who warned me not to get my hopes up. "Very rarely is anyone released after their first hearing," he said. Nevertheless, I was bolstered by his impression of Ruby's brother. Sam's record over the past fifteen years had been spotless. According to the case manager, Sam had stayed out of trouble and worked hard around the prison, using his plumbing and electrician skills to keep the prison in repair. He had also earned his GED, taking every class available to him. He used his free time to create paintings and leather items and cards for Ruby. They showed his artistic talent and his love for his sister.

I was certain all these commendations regarding his behavior would be enough to warrant parole.

I picked up Ruby and Lizzie Lou for another trip to Buena Vista just nine months after our first excursion. The parole hearing could start as early as 9:00 a.m. or as late as 3:00 p.m.

During our drive, I was naively hopeful. I thought about how I would reiterate what I said in my letters and tell the parole board how much Ruby needed her brother's help and how it was my understanding he had been a model prisoner. I also thought about how I would tell them about Ruby's poor health. Ruby's doctor had given us a detailed letter listing all of her current and very serious medical conditions. I made copies and brought them with me to give to each board member. I would tell them my husband and I were respectable members of the community and we would sponsor him. We had no idea what that would involve, but Bruce and I had talked it over, prayed about it, and came to the conclusion if this was something God wanted us to do, He would help us do it.

Because it was December, I thought I might talk about how wonderful it would be for the board to give Ruby and her brother the gift of spending Christmas together.

I had so many great ideas, I was sure they would see how sound my reasoning was. Surely, they would agree that granting parole was the right thing to do. This man had served nineteen years, after all!

Ruby and I arrived at the prison at 8:00 a.m. We were early, so we sat in the car rehearsing my speech. I didn't badger Ruby about her multiple cigarettes. She settled Lizzie Lou in her dog bed with blankets and water, cracked the windows, and ordered her to behave.

The line started forming for visitors and parole hearing participants at 8:45. While we were waiting, a family member of another inmate pointed out to me that my phone, water bottle, and handbag would not be allowed in the visitor's area. I left the line to take all the contraband back to the car. When I came back, the people that had been around us in line were nice enough to have saved my place.

As soon as we got inside, we were given lockers for our coats and car keys.

So many rules!

This was before 9/11, so I was a bit taken aback by the metal detector and felt incredibly violated by the pat down. The tube of lipstick in my pocket set off the device. I could sense the other visitors thinking, "rookie." Ruby knew the drill and patiently waited for me to pass inspection.

Next, we were escorted to the "canteen." We sat at tables and stared at the vending machines, which we couldn't use since our quarters were safely locked in the car.

Guards kept coming in and out of a door, bringing inmates to sit at tables across from their visitors. I felt as if I were having an out-of-body experience. I looked around the stark visitor's room. This was a room full of Rubys—broken families, broken dreams, broken promises, broken lives—all because someone they cared about had broken a law, or at least had been convicted of doing so.

I wondered about their stories, the reasons behind their crimes. Were some of the inmates innocent like Ruby believed her brother to be? I felt some sort of strange companionship with everyone in that room with us. I was surrounded by incarcerated felons and their families. I didn't know their crimes, I didn't know their victims, I only saw *their* hurting children and families. I know it was their victims who deserved my sympathy, but sitting in that room, I felt overwhelmed by sadness and compassion for them.

At last, a guard came in a different door and announced Ruby's brother's name and told us to follow him through another set of doors, down a long hallway. We were ushered into another room and given seats across from a table where three people were seated. Their chairs were facing us, but they were all turned sideways chatting with each other, ignoring our presence.

Ruby and I sat holding hands in silence when a man with a long, gray beard, wearing an orange jumpsuit and shackles was escorted into the room by an armed guard. He passed in front of us and said, "Hi, Sis." Ruby reached out to touch his hand and the guard reprimanded her saying she was not allowed to touch the prisoner. She was silently weeping.

The threesome sitting at a long table in front of us comprised the parole board—or at least part of it. Apparently, there were four more members of the board, but it was not necessary for them to be present. These three board members were to report their findings to the others and make a case for or against a second meeting with the full board of seven. Ruby's brother stood to the left of the board members with a guard standing next to him.

A gentleman board member welcomed Ruby and me and said it was the board's understanding I was going to speak on the prisoner's behalf. He informed us the hearing was being recorded.

We were told of his crime in detail and reminded how he had been convicted and sentenced to life in prison. A board member asked Ruby's brother if he was remorseful.

"Yes, Sir. I am very sorry for the victim's family," her brother answered respectfully, with hands cuffed in front of him. "But truthfully I have no memory of the crime."

Each member pressed him further, but he continued to calmly and politely state his lack of memory regarding the crime.

"You have someone you have asked to speak on your behalf today, is that correct?" another member of the panel inquired.

"Yes, that lady sitting next to my sister, Cy DeBoer. She has been helping my Sis. She has been an angel to Ruby. I'm so grateful that—"

"Mrs. DeBoer," one of the board members interrupted. "Please stand and tell us your name and your relationship to the prisoner."

"My name is Cy DeBoer, and he is the brother of my friend, Ruby," I said.

"How long have you known him?"

"Well, I don't actually *know* him, but as I wrote in my letter —did you get the letters I sent to all of you?" I queried.

"Yes, we all got your letters," the head board member replied. "If I remember correctly you've known the inmate's sister less than a year. Is that right?"

"That's right, but I've come to know her very well." Nervous, I said only a portion of what I had intended to say about my fondness for Ruby and the loving relationship she had with her brother and started right in with my talking points. "I've spoken with her brother on the phone. Ruby thinks the world of him. My husband and I are well-respected members of our community, and we'll be happy to sponsor him if he is released. His sister is ill, she needs his assistance." I spoke the points as quickly as I could get them out. I felt I would soon be cut off.

"Thank you for coming. As we have your letters and the inmate's history since his incarceration, we will take everything into account and make our decision. The inmate's case manager will inform him of our decision within the next few days."

"I am glad Ruby has found a friend, Mrs. DeBoer. Your time and interest is appreciated," a woman on the board thanked me. "Ruby, thank you as well, for appearing today on your brother's behalf. Have a safe trip home."

Ruby's brother had already been taken out in the hallway. As we walked by him, he looked at me and said, "Thank you, Cy, for watching over my sister. I love her so much. God bless you."

It only took two days to learn parole was denied. He would be eligible for another hearing in five years.

It was becoming clearer to me that I couldn't fix this. God could, but in His time not ours. But would He fix it? How long could Ruby continue to suffer this unfathomable sorrow? Did her brother really do the horrible thing they said he did? Now that I'd actually met him, I cared so much more for him. Is that why God brought me here today? Was it just to expand my territory or to also expand my heart?

TWELVE

First Birthday Party

December 17, 2000, was Ruby's fifty-fifth birthday. We love to celebrate at our house. Not even Groundhog Day goes by without some observance. There was no way Ruby was going to escape a birthday party—especially after her brother's parole had been denied. I hoped it might cheer her up a tiny bit.

"Ruby, let's celebrate your birthday next week."

"What do you mean?"

"Let's have a party."

"I ain't ever had a birthday party. I'm too old to have one now."

"Never, ever?" I asked.

"No, we didn't have no parties."

"Well, it is time, then!" I declared.

It took a great deal of convincing. Ruby ran through a list of reasons a party was a bad idea: she had no friends; she was too shy; and the universal problem of every woman, she had nothing to wear.

I tried to counter all of her excuses: "Ruby, I have been

blessed with friends who will love you. We'll keep it small. Bruce, Whitney, a couple of our friends and you, of course. We will go shopping for something you would like to wear."

"I like yellow cake with chocolate frosting and vanilla walnut ice cream," she conceded.

On December 17, 2000, the night of Ruby's party, some dear neighbors joined Bruce, Whitney, Ruby, and me around our dining table. We celebrated a woman who deserved to feel loved on her birthday and be the center of attention for the first time in her life. Ruby wore her new purple sweater with a big butterfly on the front and dangling earrings her brother had made for her.

When Ruby blew out her candles, she wasn't the only one with tears in her eyes.

The joy of that moment was one of the greatest gifts any of us at the table had ever received. Even though it wasn't my birthday, I made a wish, too. I wished that Ruby would see that it was Jesus who had arranged her first birthday party, right down to the yellow cake and very hard to find vanilla walnut ice cream.

For fifty-five of Ruby's years she had not been celebrated. No packages from parents with ribbons and bows. No little friends pinning tails on a donkey or dropping clothes pins in a milk bottle. No musical chairs, no balloons, no candles, and no yellow cake. Ruby's life was changing. My life was changing. My family's life was changing. Ruby was changing us.

EIGHT DAYS later was Christmas and we had been invited to my best friend's house in Pueblo for Christmas dinner. Judy and Ross invited Ruby as well, but she could not be convinced that she wouldn't be intruding. She would not come with us no matter how hard we tried to convince her. Judy even called her, but Ruby thanked her politely and said she just wanted to stay home with Lizzie Lou.

On Christmas Eve, Bruce and I drove to Ruby's apartment and gave her a few presents and a pre-cooked turkey dinner before we left town.

We also gave her a gift from Christine and Vic, friends who had been at Ruby's birthday dinner. This generous couple had hosted a holiday dinner for their two sons' high school football team, inviting fellow athletes and their parents. In the invitation, Christine had included a note that shared a bit of Ruby's story and invited families to bring gift cards that would be passed on to Ruby. Christine and Vic had collected over $300 worth of gift cards for Ruby's Christmas.

When we gave Ruby the gift cards, she was stunned.

"Them people don't even know me, and they spent their money on me? I ain't ever heard of nothin' like it. You sure got you some nice friends."

Ruby's heart had been touched by the kindness of strangers. But what really struck me was how deeply Ruby's story was touching the hearts of others.

THIRTEEN

Cinderella Goes to the Ball

(VIA MIDLAND, TEXAS)

On January 20, 2001, President George W. Bush was to be inaugurated for his first term as the forty-third President of the United States. Bruce and I were invited to attend the balls and festivities surrounding the inaugural event prior to the swearing-in ceremony.

Despite the excitement of attending a real ball, I was worried because this would be the first time I would leave town for any length of time since Ruby had come into my life.

It was on one of our Ruby Tuesdays, while we were at one of her favorite restaurants—a $6.99 all-you-can-eat Chinese buffet—that I broke the news to Ruby.

Her plate on the cafeteria tray was piled high with every deep-fried item available and a tall glass of milk. As she started eating, I decided to "bite the wonton" and proceed with the news.

"Hey, Ruby, I am leaving town for a few days.

"Are you coming back?" She put down her fork.

"Of course, I'll be gone less than I week, like I said, silly."

"Where are you going?"

"You're not going to like it," I confessed. "I am going to President Bush's inauguration in Washington, DC." I knew she would be unimpressed. Ruby often declared her dislike of politicians, especially during that endless election season.

"Them politicians are all alike. They just want to steal your money. Taxes are so high nobody can afford to live!"

"Ruby, you don't even pay taxes, and all politicians are not alike. I voted for President Bush, and I am excited to be going to Washington. I've never been there before."

"I'm gonna go get me some more of them dumplings." She grabbed her cane and her handbag.

"Can I watch your handbag for you? It's kind of hard to carry a tray while holding a cane and carrying thirty pounds of quarters over your shoulder," I teased.

"Alright, just make sure no one takes it," she huffed.

"It will be right here with mine. If someone comes and wants to take a handbag, I'll give them mine first," I smiled.

"You're just being funny, right?"

"Trying to be," I said with a wink. "And while you there, grab me an eggroll, okay?"

While Ruby was gone piling up another plate, I reflected on the circumstances that had culminated in Bruce and me being invited to a presidential inauguration.

The whole thing had started one night in 1997. Bruce and I were alone at the dinner table in our home in Littleton, Colorado.

"Honey, would you please pass me the salt and pepper?" I asked. "Where did you say we've been asked to move for a job?"

"Midland, Texas."

"Midland, Texas?" I thought a moment. "Isn't that where that little girl, Jessica, fell down a well in her backyard?"

"You have such a weird memory, Cy. Yes, I have been offered a job in Midland."

"In that case, never mind the salt and pepper, please pass me a gun." I was joking, of course. Sort of.

Turns out, Bruce had been offered a job as general counsel for Tom Brown, Inc., a company based in Midland, Texas. It was under extreme duress that we thought about leaving colorful Colorado for a West Texas dusty town located in Tornado Alley.

Whitney, about to begin fourth grade, tried to get the parents of her best friend to adopt her. I tried to get my friends to adopt me. Our son, Ryan, was beginning his first year of college at Colorado University. He didn't have to try to get adopted. He would get to stay where the buffalo roam while Bruce, Whitney, and I were going to where the armadillo meander.

We moved in August.

We flew in the Tom Brown, Inc. company plane to Midland. As we began our decent into the Midland airport, the vice president of the oil company, Bill Granberry, observed my apprehension as I looked out the window at the scenery below me.

He admitted, "Cy, it's not much to look at unless you like the color brown."

Profound as that remark was, it was a huge understatement. Midland, Texas, was fifty shades of brown.

Later I would tell my Colorado friends that the only real color in Midland was the bright blue Walmart bags that blew around town and could be spotted caught on the thorns of mesquite bushes.

When we first moved to Texas, my mom sent me a book called *Bloom Where You're Planted* because I'd been grumbling so much about moving to Midland. The name of the book was based on 1 Corinthians 7:20: "Each person should remain in the situation [*she* was] in when God called [*her*]." I had been called (shoved?) to Texas, and while my physical location had changed, that didn't mean my calling had changed. This was my home, where I would most likely live for a long time. I figured I'd better start blooming.

Astoundingly, in a very short while, I grew to love the Midlanders and their big-as-Texas hearts. The landscape never did anything to inspire me but people sure did—and the sunsets.

We joined a great church, the First Presbyterian Church of Midland. We were amazed by the empty streets on Sundays. Everyone was in church. People didn't ask *if* you went to church; they asked *where* you went to church.

Life seemed so much simpler in Midland. We were used to a much faster pace in Denver. It took us awhile to adjust to the slower place.

On Sundays we left far too early for church, with no traffic to delay our arrival.

When we made reservations at restaurants, bewildered hostesses would call the manager to see if that was even a thing.

We went to Rock Hound minor league baseball games and loved the fifties atmosphere.

They even had a hockey team in Odessa, the Jackalopes. Compared to the Colorado Avalanche, the Stanley Cup champions at the time, the Texas hockey games were a riot to watch. Not the athletes, but the fans, who were new to the sport.

Their football genes were "Friday Night Lights" deep, their hockey genes, not so much. The new fans were always yelling things like "Get the ball!" and asking, "when's halftime?" I'm sure this has long since changed but at the time it provided us with more than a few grins.

I joined a Bible study, as it was such a huge part of my life in Colorado and one of the hardest things for me to leave behind. Whitney got involved in soccer and basketball—the same sports she had played in Colorado. But in Midland the grass was very sparse (non-existent) on the soccer field and the temperature was in the nineties. The hot wind felt like it blew ninety miles an hour. Bruce and I picked up where we left off in Denver, on the sidelines for every game.

Having just written a little book called *Take a Woman's Word for It*, a dictionary according to women, I had a few Barnes and Noble book signings and became the speaker du jour for all the women's groups. It was a fun way to meet people.

As my contacts and friends grew, God encouraged me to begin an outreach for women and children. My association with the Gathering Place in Colorado had such a special place in my heart, and I missed that part of my life. One of the things I'd done in Littleton was put a bin on our front porch and asked neighbors to drop items in it that would be of help to the women and children at the Gathering Place.

Now, in Midland, I thought I'd take my collection bin idea a bit bigger. (We were in Texas after all!) Soon my amazing new Midland neighbors got involved, and we started reaching out to other neighborhoods. Between my speaking gigs and some ambitious kindhearted friends, we grew quickly. We called our neighborhood collections Bin Blessed. We gave our donations of toys, clothing, and home making supplies to Safe Haven and the Permian Basin Women's Crisis Center.

Barely two years after we'd arrived, I had two unexpected

life changing events: My mother passed away in her sleep in Colorado in June 1999, and in August of that same year we learned the Tom Brown Corporation was moving their head-quarters—and us!—back to Colorado. I was despondent over my mother's death, because she had died alone. I was also unhappy about returning to Colorado. I had come to love Midland, Texas.

IT WAS HARD TO BELIEVE, but I'd actually turned into a Texan wannabe. I loved the southern drawl: Saying "all y'all" made me sound like a native Texan.

Also, as it happened, Midland was no longer known as the town where "Baby Jessica" fell down the well. It was then the home of Texas governor George W. Bush. In fact, he had been a member of the Tom Brown Inc. board of directors. and his best friend and campaign manager for his Texas run for governor was Bruce's boss, Don Evans. About the time we left Midland and moved back to Colorado, "W" decided to run for President, which is how several of Bruce's coworkers, plus Bruce and I, had landed once-in-a-lifetime opportunities to attend a couple of the presidential inaugural balls: Black Tie and Boots and the Texas-Wyoming.

Not that I had anything appropriate to wear. Just like Cinderella.

Thankfully, I had a very well-dressed fairy godmother for a friend. Rhonda outfitted me from her closet filled with furs and gowns. She was not just a fashion fairy; this godmother had a no-nonsense wisdom. Rhonda was the significant influence on my changing my attitude toward moving to Midland in the first place. She was one of my friends I had whined to about this terrible move my husband was considering before asking for asylum at her house. She denied my request and told me to get my butt to Texas with my husband where I belonged and knock off the whining because she knew I adored Bruce, and it was all a ploy to get people to feel sorry for me. Hmm, I told you she was wise.

MY MUSINGS CAME to a stop as Ruby returned to the table.

And she had even remembered my eggroll!

"So you're friends with the President?" she asked as if it were no surprise for an angel to be friends with a President.

"No, but the boss of the company Bruce works for is a good friend of the President. That's how we ended up being invited."

"Can you mail me a postcard? I ain't seen Washington, and I ain't gettin' on no plane to do it. Ever! I'm terrified of flying."

"Have you ever flown?"

"Nah, they'd have to knock me out."

I wasn't surprised, remembering how challenging it was for Ruby to ride an elevator.

"Sure, I'll send you a postcard of the White House."

"I'd rather have a picture of somethin' else," Ruby said bluntly, adding, "I've seen the White House on the news."

"Alright, maybe I can find you a postcard with animals grazing on the White House lawn."

"Yeah, that would be good." She really seemed to like that idea.

Before I took Ruby home, we ran a few errands. It was snowing outside, and I'd suggested she not use her scooter as a snowplow, so I was glad to help her stock up on a few groceries. When we got to the checkout stand, buried under the cans of Mighty Dog were ten giant Hershey bars.

"Ruby! What is with the candy bars? Have you forgotten

what your doctor said? Please put them back. I don't want you to go into a diabetic coma while I am gone!"

"They were ten for five bucks! I promise, I'll eat only one square a day."

"Oh, Ruby, you are killing me. Actually, you're killing you!" I chastised.

We unloaded her groceries, and I hugged her goodbye.

"If you don't come back, I'll understand, but I'll always love you. I won't forget what you done for me and my brother."

"Ruby, I am coming back! I'll beat your postcards back, and we will have lots of pictures to show you. Please trust me, I would never just leave and not return. Jesus won't let me. Remember, He is the one running our show." It was important to keep reminding her it was never about me.

"Okay, but if you don't come back, I'll understand."

Before I left, I gave Ruby the phone number of my friend Sue who would be able to help Ruby while I was away.

WHEN BRUCE and I landed at Reagan National Airport, it was the beginning of a fantasy weekend.

The experience cast a bright light on the monumental disparities in Ruby's life and mine. Since the day God chose me to be Ruby's friend, all good things that happened to me after meeting Ruby made me ask, "Why me, Lord? Why not Ruby?"

I asked that question a lot while we were in Washington.

I thought about my mother often during the trip too. For instance, when Bruce and I looked over our shoulders and discovered we were sitting a few rows in front of Colin Powell during the opening ceremonies at the Lincoln Memorial, we couldn't believe it.

I said aloud as if she could hear me, "Mom, how crazy is

this? In front of Colin Powell? You love Colin Powell! Are you seeing this?"

Along with our Tom Brown friends, we were pretty much in awe of our circumstances. I don't think I'd be wrong if I said we all were wondering how we ever ended up in those coveted seats. There were thousands of people on the Washington Mall, standing behind us as far as we could see.

I was awestruck by the inspiring memorial to my favorite, and my mom's as well, president: Abraham Lincoln. My mother loved being an American and was the most patriotic woman I have ever known. I have a very old and faded black and white photo of her at age three waving an American flag in front of her house in Monte Vista, Colorado. Red, white, and blue ran through her veins. It runs through mine too.

Unlike Ruby, I grew up with a mother who made certain her children understood what a privilege it is to live in America, and never to forget the men who fought to keep us free. I have a memory box with letters my mom wrote to Everett Dirksen and Ronald Reagan, along with their responses. She had written a beautiful patriotic poem she wanted to share with them. It's about why each state in this union is worth fighting for. It is entitled "50 Good Reasons."

Conversely, Ruby's mother left her with nothing to believe in or trust about America or otherwise. Ruby deserved a mother like mine as much as I did.

The opening ceremony Wednesday night was filled with patriotism, entertainers, speakers, and cheering. It was freezing, but for once in my life, I didn't complain about the cold. My goose bumps were not from the temperature.

We were DC tourists by day, guests of the Inaugural Committee by night.

The following night we were the Committee's guests at their very lively Texan party featuring ZZ Top!

Friday night when we attended the Black Tie and Boots Ball, it felt like we were back in Texas. Even Bevo, the Texas University mascot, was in attendance along with an array of Country Western entertainers. Bruce in his tuxedo and I in my gown danced in the crowded ballroom stepping all over each other's cowboy boots!

The following cold and rainy morning we were taken in private buses to the inauguration of George W. Bush, the forty-third President of the United States. The same buses drove us down the middle of the parade route complete with a police escort. We had a box lunch waiting on our bus seats with the presidential seal on them. *Really, who were we?* We were delivered to the parade viewing stands right next to where the Bushes and our friends Don and Susie Evans were seated.

Ball gown number two was unveiled for the Texas Wyoming Ball that night. Of course, the Bushes and the Cheneys made appearances, which excited the rowdy crowd. They were now the official First Families.

Still, nothing during the weekend could have topped Sunday morning at the National Cathedral. We sat about five rows behind the Bushes during the beautiful service at which Franklin Graham preached. It was a beautiful service filled with reverence and grace.

It's amazing where Jesus will take you if you are willing. Sure, you may have to go through the desert first—or at least Midland.

Bruce and I were very aware Who had orchestrated this weekend for us. Jesus had sent us to Midland, and He honored our faithfulness to bloom where we were planted by treating us to an epic experience of a lifetime.

We sent Ruby a postcard every day. Only one had arrived before we got home. It is not easy to find animal postcards in Washington, DC, so I had to throw in a few of the monuments.

FOURTEEN

"Whatcha Doin'?"

---

*A*lmost every morning my home phone would ring. I would answer, and the caller would greet me with the question, "Whatcha doin'?"

I didn't need caller ID to know who it was.

I've always hated this question any time of the day, but especially first thing in the morning. It makes me feel guilty. I always feel like I should have an answer that is much more impressive than the truth. Most of the time my 7:00 a.m. wake-up calls from Ruby embarrassed me because I had to confess that I was in bed, and she'd already been up for several hours. (In my defense I was typically up reading past midnight, while Ruby went to bed around 8 p.m.)

At first, I tried just letting it ring, so I could simply go back to sleep. But my irritating conscience wouldn't allow such an indulgence. After the phone stopped ringing, I'd be lying there in bed, trying to count sheep, when I would start imagining the worst (as if she were one of my kids!), and then I'd call her back within a few minutes.

Exasperated by the painfully regularity of the way-too-early calls on my home line, I stopped calling her back. If she calls back on my cell, I reasoned, then I'll take her call. Eventually I started to let the cell phone go unanswered, too, and waited until the home phone began to ring again. That was the rule I made for myself. Three calls and I had to pick up.

"Hi, Cy, it's Ruby. Whatcha doin'?"

"Nothing, Ruby, what are you up to?" As the words left my mouth, it dawned on me that I was doing little more than rephrasing "Whatcha doin'?" I guess I have an equally annoying query in my quiver.

"Just callin' to see if you was gonna be in the neighborhood today." She never did seem to understand the distance between our homes and how slight the chance was of my being in her neighborhood.

"Sorry, Ruby I'm not. Are you okay? Do you need something?"

"Nah, I just thought if you was around we might go to Arch or somethin'. I got me a prescription ready at Walgreens but my scooter ain't running that great. Some kids was yellin' at me from their car windows yesterday. They called me an old witch and said I should be ridin' a broom instead of my slow sorry scooter."

Lord, why do some people have to be so mean?

"Oh, Ruby, you know what? I *will* be in the neighborhood, actually. Let's go to ARC and lunch."

That was one of those "Whatcha doin'?" calls I am glad I answered. God knew Ruby could use a touch of kindness, and truthfully, what else did I really have to do that was more important? In God's eyes, nothin'.

"Glad you wasn't busy when I called. I been feelin' kinda blue," Ruby said as she locked the door behind her.

"I'm sorry, what's goin' on?"

"Ah, nothin'. Just feelin' so tired. I called the doctor to see if he could up my depression medicine. I ain't heard back yet."

"What sounds good for lunch?" I asked, wishing I had a better solution for her. "Mexican or Chinese?" Food Tourette's strikes again.

"I think you like that Chinese buffet better than Mexican," she guessed. She'd guessed wrong, darn it.

"Chinese it is!" I smiled, knowing it was her favorite.

As always, she was upset with the no to-go box policy since after several trips to the buffet she ended up with some leftovers on her plate.

"I don't get why we can't take a box home with us if they call it 'all you can eat'," she complained as usual. "I can eat more later tonight; I just can't eat it all this minute. Sounds like false advertising to me."

"I know. We should talk to a lawyer."

Ruby did seem a bit off her game when we started browsing around ARC. Usually she liked to go down every aisle and pick things up and check out their prices. Then she'd declare "Rip off!" or "That's a pretty good deal" and move on to the next item that caught her eye. Today, she didn't pick up anything. We just looked at a few tops and the jewelry.

"I think I'm ready to go back to the apartment," she announced after a while.

"That's fine. Are you feeling alright?" I asked, wondering if she looked a little pale.

"I'll be fine; just a little tired."

I took her home, and she perked up when she realized she hadn't missed *Oprah*. "You go on home, Cy. I don't like you getting' caught up in traffic."

"Call me if you need anything." I hugged her goodbye.

When Ruby called the next morning, she finally admitted what had been on her mind.

"I ain't heard from my brother in a few weeks. I got my check and sent a few dollars to put on his books, so he could get some food from them vending machines. He can't eat that food up there; it gets him sick. I'm so worried about him. He is so worn down. I been tellin' him how you are a Christian, and he wondered if you had an extra Bible you could send him." She said all that without drawing a breath. She'd been hanging around me too long.

"Of course, do they let him get packages?"

"Yeah, but they have to come direct from a store not a person. So I guess you can't just send him an extra one of yours."

"No problem, we have a bookstore at our church. I'll have a Bible mailed from there," I said, adding, "but I do have several extra Bibles. I can give one of them to you, if you'd like."

"Nah," she said. "My favorite book is the dictionary."

"Really? I never knew that. I think you might get a lot out of the Bible too, though."

"Cy, I can't understand the Bible. Maybe after I read the dictionary some more, I'll be able to. I only learn one new word a day, so I doubt if I have enough time to read both."

Was she being funny or serious? My guess was serious, but I wanted to laugh.

"Ruby, there are Bibles that are easier to read than others. There are some with Jesus's words written in red in the New Testament. We can find one that is simpler to understand. I use a Study Bible and I also read a Bible called *The Message*, which is written more in a story form. Let's get you one of those."

"Nah, you can just tell me what the Bible says. I like it better when I hear it from you."

"What are you doing on Sunday?" I asked.

"Nothin'. Whatcha doin'?"

"Taking you to church."

FIFTEEN

Next of Kin

*B*ruce and I were looking forward to taking Ruby to church. We researched the church website to make sure the sermon wasn't going to be on tithing. We were a bit nervous that she would be intimidated by the size of our congregation. We attend Cherry Hills Community Church in Highlands Ranch, Colorado. I warned her that a lot of people attended our church.

"If we can sit in the back, I'll go," Ruby agreed, setting her terms. "I want to be able to get out of there if I don't like it."

I called her on Sunday morning to remind her of our church plans before we drove the forty-five minutes to pick her up.

Her phone rang and rang. I usually gave her about ten rings since she might be out walking Lizzie Lou and not have her cell with her.

Twenty rings and still no answer.

I hung up, waited a few minutes, and tried again.

Still no answer.

I kept trying both her phones every five minutes for about

half an hour. I was getting more anxious as time was growing short for us to make it to her house and back to church on time.

"I don't know what to do. Should we just go get her?" I asked Bruce. "I don't know any neighbors to call who might check on her. What do you think?"

"Try the manager's office. Maybe they can send someone to knock on her door."

"Good idea," I said, already picking up my phone. A moment later, a voice mail message informed me the office didn't open until noon on Sundays.

My imagination immediately started leading me down the most dreadful paths. Bruce recognized the trajectory my thoughts were taking and suggested we head to Ruby's apartment regardless.

Just then my phone rang.

When I answered, I heard an unfamiliar voice.

"May I speak with Cy DeBoer?"

"This is she."

"I'm a charge nurse at St. Anthony's Hospital, and I am calling on behalf of Ruby Jean. She has listed you as her next of kin."

"Is she alright?" I asked, panic rising. "Is she in the hospital? What happened?"

"She is in a room right now. She came into emergency by ambulance late last night. She is stable and asking for you. She is very agitated and doesn't want to cooperate unless you are here with her. Do you live with her or near here? We need to ask you a few questions about her medical history. She is also very worried about her dog."

"I can be there in about forty-five minutes," I said, grabbing my keys and handbag. "Tell her I am on my way and that she needs to cooperate. Can you put her on the phone?"

"No, they will be coming for her to run some tests, so it's best if you just get here."

Traffic was lighter than usual since it was Sunday, and I made it to the hospital in just over half an hour. I got her room number from the information desk and went to the elevator bank and began frantically pushing the up button, willing the elevator doors to open faster.

When I got to Ruby's room, I found her propped up on her pillows with her head lolled to the side, fast asleep. Her hair was down. Until now, I'd only seen her hair in braids or in a bun on top of her head. It was longer than I thought—a good six inches past her shoulders. She looked so worn, little, and lonely.

I sat on a chair by her bed and watched her sleep. Eventually, a nurse came in and we stepped outside to talk in the hallway.

"You must be Cy. I'm Elizabeth. We spoke on the phone a little while ago."

"Yes, thank you for getting in touch with me. I was worried because she hadn't answered her phone this morning when I called to remind her we were picking her up for church. I was getting a little panicky when you called. What's wrong with her?"

"She called 911 about eleven o'clock last night. She had very high blood pressure and was complaining of chest pains when the ambulance brought her in. She was also pretty dehydrated," Elizabeth explained. "Can you tell us if she has any history of heart problems? Do they run in your family? If you could help us fill out her medical information and give us her primary physician's name, it would be helpful. She was so agitated, which isn't good with hypertension. But she just kept saying you would come help her if we called."

"I'm not sure how helpful I can be. I don't really know a lot about her medical history," I admitted. "But I can give you her doctor's name and the few conditions I know about. We aren't related, but I am her best friend. Her only friend."

Realizing how peculiar it sounded to be the best friend of someone you knew so little about, I proceeded to tell Elizabeth an abbreviated version of how Ruby and I had found each other.

"Oh, my that's quite a story," Elizabeth said, looking at me thoughtfully. "You really *are* her guardian angel then."

"Not really, Jesus is the reason we became friends. I just wish He had supplied me with a little more background information. I don't want to wake her, but I'll get her apartment key so I can take her dog out for a walk and give her some food and water. If she wakes up, will you tell her where I've gone and that I'll be back soon?"

"Of course. I think the issue with her dog is the most worrisome for her. She only talks about you and . . . is it Lizzie?"

"It's Elizabeth Louise, but you can call her Lizzie Lou."

I went back into Ruby's room as her eyes began to flutter open.

As soon as she saw me, she said, "Cy, is that you? I told 'em all here you would come. I don't think they believed me. They been poking me with all kinds of needles and asking me a bunch of questions. I just want outa here. I need to go take care of Lizzie Lou. She is goin' to be scared."

Ruby was sitting up now and tossing her bare feet over the side of the bed. Those little feet missing two toes, and her slippers—I wanted her to have those toes and slippers.

"Ruby, I was worried about you. We were planning on

taking you to church today, and when I called to remind you, there was no answer."

"Bet you thought I left town so I wouldn't have to go to church," she said, giving me one of her impish grins.

"It crossed my mind. But seriously what happened? How are you feeling?"

"Well, you know how my doctor keeps warning me about having a heart attack or stroke 'cause of my smokin'," she confessed reluctantly. "I figured that was what was happening last night, so I called me an ambulance."

"I'm so glad you called and got yourself here in time. And, no, I didn't know your doctor has been warning you about heart attacks and strokes. You told me he was treating you for anxiety, depression, and diabetes. But the stroke and heart attack risks make sense with all the cigarettes you smoke," I said, clearly aggravated.

When I heard how judgmental I sounded, I tried to soften my voice, adding, "I am so sorry you had to have such a frightening experience, Ruby. I would have been terrified. Why don't I go take care of Lizzie Lou? Then I'll come back and visit some more. In the meantime, try to answer the nurses' questions the best you can, and be more affable. That's your new dictionary word for the day," I said, and we both laughed.

Ruby gave me her keys and all the warnings and instructions necessary to enter her apartment and not frighten Lizzie Lou. I was more frightened of Lizzie Lou than she was of me. Her mood could change on a dime. Some days she liked me, other days not very much.

It didn't take long to get to Ruby's place. I parked and walked to the stoop, pausing before unlocking the door. "Good girl, Lizzie Lou," I consoled from my side of the door. "I'm coming in to feed you. Won't that be nice? I bet you're hungry."

Her growling intensified along with scratching.

"Your mom sent me. She is worried about you. I'm coming in." I slowly opened the door hoping she wouldn't escape and wishing I could.

"Hi, Lizzie Lou, you remember me, right? I'm Aunt Cy; your mom's friend—and next of kin. You should know me by now. I know you haven't been alone with me much. I'm very nice, an angel actually, so shall we feed you?" I sounded like a contestant in a Miss Congeniality contestant.

It worked! Lizzie Lou stood down. She let me pass and walk to her bowl. I filled it with dog food, and while she ate ravenously, I cleaned up a few of her accidents around the apartment.

When she finished eating, I gingerly hooked the leash to her collar, and she took me for a walk. It felt like she could pull a sled. Lizzie Lou immediately had six feet of taut leash between us and dragged me to her favorite relief station. She continued to steer me through the meandering apartment complex and eventually back to her front door. I gave her a few pats of reassurance and laid a jacket of Ruby's near Lizzy Lou's dog bed for comfort. I think we left our relationship in better standing.

Ruby was released the next day with the requisite follow-up discharge papers, instructions, and a few more prescriptions to add to her ever-growing collection of pill bottles. She was also given a strict verbal admonishment from the attending physician to stop smoking and to maintain a heathier diet. Pamphlets from the American Lung, Heart and Diabetes Associations were stapled to the discharge form.

I took her home, then went to fill her prescriptions and shop for some healthy groceries. When I got back to Ruby's place with the groceries and meds, she informed me of all the mistakes they made in the hospital, and I reminded her to follow the doctor's orders and call me if she needed anything.

When I left for my house, Ruby was propped on her couch eating low-sodium chicken noodle soup and a sandwich. She was relieved she'd made it home in time for both *Oprah* and *Dr. Phil*—and if she could stay awake, *Wheel of Fortune*.

She and Rain Man would have made excellent roommates.

I called her later that evening to check on her. After she thanked me for my help, she said, "*Affable* means: pleasant, easy to approach and talk to; friendly, cordial, warmly polite. Night, Cy, I love you."

"Good night, next of kin."

SIXTEEN

Plan B

———

"Ey, it's me, Ruby. Whatcha doin'?"

"Hi Ruby, haven't heard from you in a while. I'm sitting at my desk working on my Bible study for this week. It's about the fruit of the Spirit. I'm trying to figure out my spiritual gifts."

"You know how I been wantin' to get my driver's license? Well, I got me a car!" Ruby announced, unconcerned with my spiritual gift, which now I wished were patience.

I sat in stunned silence.

"I just got a few more papers to sign and a favor to ask ya," she said, ignoring my silence.

"Ruby, you don't even have a license, yet. How can you drive a car? How did you find a car and the money to pay for it? Ruby, I can't lie, I am shocked."

"I rode my scooter over to that dealer always advertising on TV that they don't need nothin' down and can make credit arrangements. The fellow there was real nice. I told him how I need a car with good tires and engine to go visit my brother. So I got me a station wagon. It's in real good shape, just a few scratches and dents. The upholstery is nice up front, and I can just lay me a blanket down in the back."

"Ruby, do you realize the cost of insurance? Gas? Maintenance?" I sounded like the mother of a sixteen-year-old.

"I talked to a nice lady at State Farm, and she can get me a policy for a good price. The salesman told me it should run fine for quite a while, and other than oil changes, I shouldn't have any trouble."

I was impressed with Ruby's initiative to get the car and the insurance quote. She had been very lethargic and unmotivated lately, but now she sounded as animated as I had ever heard her in the three years I'd known her. I didn't like the false hope the salesman had planted, but I didn't want to diminish her sense of accomplishment either.

While Ruby had been talking about getting her license and a car for a long time, Bruce and I had agreed that a car was the last thing she needed. While she was very conscientious about her spending, her disability income was just over seven hundred dollars per month and her rent, utilities, and groceries left her with little extra—most of which she sent to her brother.

Bruce and I helped her a bit here and there, but she wouldn't take much. We had her on our phone plan, and sometimes she'd let me pay for a few groceries. Other than that, I had to resort to hiding a few twenties in her purse or showing up at her house with a bag of food and a fabricated story that I'd needed to use up a bunch of coupons before they expired. She turned down lots of offers from me to take her shopping.

In other words, Ruby was very independent. She never asked for money and rarely for favors, unless it was for her brother or transportation.

"Ruby," I said, "you mentioned you had a favor to ask. What favor?"

"I've been saving for a year, and I have seven hundred dollars in the bank. I was wondering if I could give you that and borrow the rest to pay the car dealer. Then I'll pay you back every month. I promise I'll pay every cent, and I want you to charge me interest."

This was obviously difficult for her to ask.

"I will check with Bruce, but I think we would both feel better if we had more time to help you look for a car *after* you get your license."

"I been checkin' on cars for a long time. I got me a friend here at the apartments who is a mechanic, and he says he'll look it over for me. I know this car is a good deal. It runs good. I drove it around the block."

I heard such desperation and hope in her voice that I ignored the part about her driving around the block with no license. I told her I would talk to Bruce and let her know.

"Thank you, Cy. Tell Bruce thank you. The guy at the lot said he'd hold it for twenty-four hours."

You can imagine my next call.

"Bruce, honey, guess what?"

Against his better instincts, Bruce once again let his heart lead him in the hopes that two things might happen: first, that Ruby could become less dependent, and second, that I could become more independent.

Bruce bought the car and turned the title over to Ruby. She made him write up an agreement for her to pay us fifty dollars monthly to us. This was for her peace of mind, to "make it legal."

"I feel better knowing we got us a contract," she said. "I promise I'm gonna make my payments."

I began to affectionately refer to Bruce as Plan B for Bruce. The man certainly knew how to make things happen.

. . .

In time, I began to see a pattern. As hard as I tried to make Ruby's life easier, it seems eventually she'd sabotaged herself. She thought she was doing something independent and brilliant, but that was not always the case.

Frequently, she would make a decision for herself, and then bring me into the loop when the loop was hopelessly knotted. Purchasing a car had all the markings of that kind of situation. Luckily it worked out alright, but a few months later, Ruby unintentionally created a complete mess with her disability and social security benefits that not even Plan B could untangle.

The whole thing started when Ruby learned that her ex-husband had died and, without telling anyone, decided to file for his social security. The additional income she received wasn't much, but when she reported it on her disability form, it set the wheels of government into motion. Apparently with her ex-husband's additional social security, she exceeded her allowed income by about fifty-eight dollars. Suddenly her disability checks stopped coming and Medicaid stopped paying for her medications. Without Medicaid, she couldn't afford the incredible expense of over fifteen prescriptions. So she just stopped taking them.

The first I heard of any of this was after she had been without the medication for three months. It took almost eight months and two conferences with a judge to get her disability and Medicaid monthly checks restored. To help Ruby, the judge enlisted the help of the Pickle Rule. Apparently, it is a real thing, which is great because if ever anyone was in a pickle, it was Ruby.

The Pickle Rule is named after former US Representative James ("Jake") Pickle who, in 1976, objected to an annual Cost of Living Allowance (COLA) for Social Security benefits because that small increase in income would cost some people their Medicaid eligibility. The Pickle Rule excludes the cost of living increases from counting as income against Medicaid eligibility. The judge declared Ruby's ex's benefit as a COLA and therefore it didn't affect her Medicaid.

Before she got out of her pickle, Bruce sent Ruby money to help her pay for the medicine she needed. She was overwhelmed with gratitude, and I was once again reminded how blessed I am to have the gift of Bruce as my husband.

Then there was the car repair fiasco. When Ruby's car broke down, she called someone her brother had known in prison. She gave him three hundred dollars and let him take the car to his "garage." Ruby called him daily, and he always said the same thing: he was a little behind but promised the car would be ready soon. After three weeks, he told her he needed another four hundred dollars for parts. Desperate, Ruby finally called me.

"Cy, I hate callin' ya, but I got myself in a bind. I need some money to pay this guy to get my car fixed. He won't give it back until he gets the money." She filled me in on the details.

"You're not giving this guy another dime, Ruby. When you gave it to him, was it drivable?"

"Yeah, a friend of his brought him to the house, so he could drive it to his garage and fix it. It was making a loud sound. I thought it might be the rotors." She explained.

"What do you know about rotors, may I ask?" I was genuinely interested.

"I know they make noise when they ain't workin' right."

"Okay, well, we also have a friend who is a mechanic. Let's get the car back and take it to him," I suggested.

Operation Recover the Taurus Wagon began. I picked Ruby up at dusk for our reconnaissance mission. We looked like Cagney and Lacey without the guns and attitude.

She had the address of the pseudo and possibly psycho mechanic. It was in a sketchy area of town. We slowly drove up to stake out the house with the headlights turned off, so we wouldn't draw any attention. The Taurus was parked in the front yard, a patch of dirt that apparently doubled as a "garage." Our plan was to use Ruby's spare keys and take the car, hoping it would run well enough to make our escape. It didn't take long to see our scheme obviously wouldn't work. The car was up on blocks with no wheels, and a Doberman was tied to a stake in the yard next to it. At least no one could steal it, not even us.

I called Plan B, who scolded us for even considering Plan A.

Bruce made some calls, and within a few days he had recovered the car and paid for repairs with a real mechanic.

Cagney and Lacey or Lucy and Ethel? You be the judge.

YET ANOTHER FINE mess comes to mind.

One day someone left a box on Ruby's door-step. It contained three tiny kittens.

"Hi, Cy. Whatcha doin'?"

This was not a call to ask my advice about the abandoned kittens. No, that ship had sailed. Ruby had already brought them in to her apartment and named them Kittycat 1, Kittycat 2, and Kittycat 3. She had also purchased a giant litter box and case of Tender Vittles along with collars.

She was merely calling to ask if I knew of a veterinarian who would give them shots at a discount, along with a rabies shot for Lizzie Lou. I don't know if this was a preventative measure in the event Lizzie Lou should bite a kitten or what.

Of course, had Ruby called me sooner, 1, 2 and 3 would have been pictured on signs posted around the complex saying, "Free Kittens."

Ruby kept the kittens. Sometimes not even a phone call to Plan B can help.

SEVENTEEN

White Knuckles

---

*G*ot car. . . need license.

The week after she got her Taurus Wagon, Ruby called me determined to take her driver's test. She told me she had been studying every day. "Sometimes right through my afternoon TV shows," she admitted. She was sure she could pass the test. Besides, since she had a learner's permit, she'd been practicing by hauling around neighbors who had licenses but no car and needed rides for various errands.

When I wondered aloud if these neighbors were taking advantage of Ruby, she told me they were all her friends, and it was a good way for her to practice driving. Besides, she felt good that she could help someone else.

I called my good friend Martha, who knew Ruby, and asked her if she would be willing to go with me to take Ruby to the Motor Vehicle Driver's License Bureau in North Denver. Martha had been to lunch with Ruby and even visited her in the hospital one time when I was out of town.

"It will be fun, Marth. Since you've met her, she feels comfortable with you."

"Has she ever driven a car?" Martha asked. "Does she even know how to drive?"

"Um, I think so. She says she's been driving her neighbors around."

"What the heck, let's do it! I'm in!" said my very good and very brave friend.

WHEN WE GOT to Ruby's place, she said she wanted to drive her own car for the test since she was more familiar with the feel of it, which was understandable. As I parked my car, Ruby, all dressed up in her favorite outfit, earrings, red nail polish, and pink bedroom slippers, climbed behind the steering wheel of her Taurus station wagon. At only five feet two inches, she had to adjust the seat forward until her face was about six inches from the steering wheel. .

I rode up front; Martha buckled into the backseat with a prayer on her lips and pallor on her face.

"Are you ready for your big day, Ruby?" Martha asked.

"Yeah, I been studying for weeks. I'm nervous, though. I'm just gonna take it slow to the place. Do either of you know how to get there?"

I had a printout of the directions on my lap, thank goodness.

"Okay, just go up here to the exit out of the complex and turn right." I looked back at poor Martha and was sure I saw white knuckles as she held the strap above the window.

Oh, so slowly, we rolled up to the exit of her apartment building. Ruby looked left, right, left again and when she was certain no cars were within miles, we crept out onto the road. Quickly, cars began to catch up with us and were passing us. There was an abundance of shaking heads and aggressive hand gestures from drivers and their passengers. Not everyone likes to go fifteen in a thirty-five-miles-per-hour zone.

"Ruby, you're doing great, but I think we need to speed it up a bit. You know, to go with the flow of traffic," I suggested.

"I ain't in no hurry. Let them pass me. I'm in the right-hand lane."

Her hands griped the wheel at ten and two. She had the focus of a sniper as she stared at the road in front of her. Thankfully, she was oblivious to many of the hand gestures. Martha and I kept exchanging looks. We weren't sure whether our situation was funny or fatal.

Twenty minutes after my direction's estimated travel time, we pulled into the DMV. Martha unbuckled her seatbelt and was out of the car in a blur. I, too, was eager to put some distance between myself and the car, but Ruby stayed put.

"Hey, Ruby," I said before leaping out of the car. "Let's go before the line gets too long."

"I ain't sure I'm ready."

"Oh, sure you are," Martha said with assurance. "You've got a great memory, and you've been studying hard."

Ruby finally got out of the car and shuffled up to the entrance where Martha had already taken a number. There were at least fifteen people in front of us.

While we had a few minutes, I asked Ruby if she had all her paperwork, including her permit, her identification card, social security card, registration for the car, insurance card, and so on. She unzipped her handbag, which resembled carry-on luggage. Reams of various sizes and slips of paper exploded from the opening. All kinds of paperwork, bank statements, and grocery receipts fell from her purse onto the floor. Martha and I started scrambling to pick them up and place them in some sort of order.

A voice spoke over a loudspeaker: "Number 34. Number 34."

"That's us, Ruby. Grab your papers, it's our turn!"

Clutching papers to our chests, Martha, Ruby, and I hurried to the window of the next available and unfortunate clerk.

"Which one of you is applying for a license?" the friendly woman asked.

"I am, but we dropped my papers so we each got a part of 'em," Ruby explained as if there was nothing unusual about the situation.

"I'm going to need your permit and your Colorado ID," the clerk explained.

The three of us began frantically working through our stacks to find those two little pieces of paper. I could feel the glare of numbers 35 through 84 boring into my back, certain the crowd would turn ugly any minute. Ruby continued to declare she knew they were "in here someplace."

"Got 'em!" Martha waived the papers like a winning lottery ticket.

Surprisingly, the clerk just smiled, gave Ruby the written test form, and pointed her to a cubicle on an adjacent wall where she could take the test. Then, seeing she had a cane, she redirected Ruby to a nearby desk.

"Good luck," the clerk said to Ruby and actually seemed to mean it.

Martha and I walked to a nearby 7-Eleven to grab a bottle of water and sit on a bench outside while we waited for Ruby to take her test. About forty-five minutes later Ruby peeked out the door, and we ran over to hear the results. She passed! Only missed one! Martha and I hugged her, and Ruby beamed.

"Now they'll call me for the driving test, when an instructor is available. They said I'd need my proof of insurance and registration. I got it in them papers somewhere."

After a lengthy search, it turned out those papers were in the glove compartment in her car.

A driving instructor called Ruby's name and she followed him out to her car while Martha and I found seats inside the DMV.

A few minutes later Ruby shuffled back inside to say the instructor wouldn't let her take the test in bedroom slippers.

"These are all I got to wear, my feet have been hurtin' and these are all I'm comfortable wearing," she said, obviously upset. "They got a rubber sole on 'em and I walk outside in these all the time. If you walk outside in 'em, they can't be called bedroom slippers."

She had a point. I felt it was one worth making with the driving instructor. I spotted him walking in from the parking lot.

"Sir, can I speak with you for a minute?" I asked as I approached. "The lady you just turned down to test, the one you said was wearing bedroom slippers? Well those aren't bedroom slippers. She wears them outside as shoes. I think you hurt her feelings by saying they weren't good enough to drive in. They are the best and most comfortable shoes she has. Please let her take the test."

He thought for a moment. "They looked like bedroom slippers to me, but if she uses them as shoes, tell her to come on and get in the car."

"Thank you! You're the best!" I gushed.

Martha and I waited anxiously for about fifteen minutes before we spotted the red bumper of Ruby's car turning into the parking lot. About thirty seconds later she completed the turn.

Ruby slowly got out of the car and told us she didn't pass. She looked so dejected.

The instructor was behind her. "She did a great job until the last turn, and she went out of turn on a four-way stop." He seemed sorry.

"When can she take it again? I immediately inquired. "It is hard for all of us to make arrangements to do this again any time soon. I live thirty miles from here, have to leave my car at her place, pick her up, wait most of the day, drive her home, then drive all the way back to my house in rush hour. It's really inconvenient. Plus, it's hard on Ruby with her health issues." I ran all the words together as I breathlessly appealed to this nice man again.

"I'll see if she can take it again later today. Why don't you go have lunch and check back in about an hour?"

After lunch, we learned she could indeed try again. We waited about forty-five more minutes as Ruby went out for round two. Martha and I prayed for her success. At last, we saw the Taurus Station wagon pull into the lot.

"She passed!" the instructor exclaimed as he jumped out of the car. Ruby opened her car door and her face had the biggest smile I'd ever seen. She was waving her certification in her hand.

Martha and I agreed we had just experienced one of our longest best days ever. We were like proud mothers riding home with our honor student. In fact, if I were driving a car sporting a bumper sticker that said: "Our honor student just passed her driver's test!" I couldn't have been prouder.

EIGHTEEN

Boundaries

---

*F*or five years I had essentially been Ruby's only friend. It wasn't always easy. In fact, at times it had been challenging to say the least. Graciously, God gave me endurance and patience I had never experienced with another person before I met Ruby. I was often amazed by my calm demeanor when I was with her. She changed me for the better in so many ways.

In our years of friendship, I sat in hospital waiting rooms after surgeries and by her bedside when she was ill. I spent many hours worrying. I accompanied her to all of her medical tests and many of her doctor visits—and held her hand for lots of elevator rides. I wrote dozens of letters to halfway houses and prison wardens and parole board members, pleading for her brother's release. I searched for available housing for him when we hoped he would be released soon.

Ruby lived her life for the sole purpose of seeing her brother released from prison. Nothing, *nothing* mattered more to her. She planned for that day and lost hope for that day, often all in the same day.

Ruby's depression and anxiety over her brother and her health were growing more and more incessant. Without explanation her brother was moved to a prison further away than Buena Vista to Sterling Correctional facility. His case manager was surprised by the move, as Sam had been a model prisoner. In the minimum-security Buena Vista facility, he'd at least had the freedom to work on his art projects and help outside the prison running heavy machinery and making repairs. This wasn't the case in the Sterling facility.

Sam called Ruby collect one night to tell her he'd been moved to Sterling, a rigid and austere place. He'd been there before and had many horrible memories of it. The story relayed to Ruby was for that some reason they thought he needed to be in a lower altitude and that the drive to Sterling would be shorter and easier for his sister. This made no sense.

A more likely explanation was that the Buena Vista facility was at capacity, and they needed to move inmates who had been convicted of more serious crimes back to the higher security prisons to make room for those convicted of lesser crimes.

Sam was devastated, and his calls to Ruby, along with her calls to me, became more frequent. I couldn't fix this. I just couldn't. Every call she made to me left me feeling helpless and inadequate. I was no longer riding the high of helpfulness. I was feeling very low, knowing I had hit a high wall—built from prison bars and bureaucracy.

At the same time Ruby needed more of my attention, it was growing harder and harder for me to carve out the time for her. My own family was going through some problems, and I needed to be there for them too. Grandma DeBoer, my sweet mother-in-law, who had met Ruby at holiday gatherings and often asked about her as Ruby did of my mother-in law, often needed help getting to the doctor or running errands. My daughter was in high school then and active in sports, and we tried to never miss a game. Our son was in Washington, DC, and we liked to visit him. I was on an advisory board for the Gathering Place and involved in their fund-raising events. I attended a weekly Bible study that required daily homework. I didn't have a paying job, but I never lacked for something to do. I was a professional volunteer, a career with job security, believe me.

My volunteering was made possible by my husband's hard work and constant encouragement. When I would apologize for always asking for him to fund my causes or half-heartedly suggest that I should perhaps get a job, he would reassure me that I had the most important job in the family: helping others.

My life had become very full—too full—and Bruce, family, and friends recognized the burnout brewing before I did. They advised I set some boundaries around Ruby. They were worried that all of Ruby's problems became my problems. Even I had to admit I dropped everything to rescue her from even minor predicaments.

Ruby never intentionally took advantage of our friendship; she just didn't know how to make friends she could count on. I provided security and comfort for her, and she wanted more of it. I didn't have the heart to let her down, but I was getting run down.

The give and take of our friendship seemed a bit one-sided. But to be honest, that was my fault; I never let her do anything for me. Ruby often offered to come make dinner for my family or to help me clean my house, but I didn't let her. I am not a gracious receiver. For some it's far more difficult to be a gracious receiver than a gracious giver. Looking back, I can see that by always giving, I took from her the opportunity to give back. I shouldn't have. It is unkind to deny others the joy of giving.

I began to wonder, "What would Jesus do?"

The truth is, He never wanted me to teach Ruby to put all her faith in *me*. He called me to teach her to put her faith in *Him*. Ruby and I had always talked a lot about Jesus. Since the day we met, I constantly reminded her not to credit me, instead to acknowledge Jesus as the one who saved her from the street. He saved her on the Cross. Any good emanating from me came from the power of Christ living in me. Not me.

But now it was time to make an adjustment, for her sake as well as for mine.

I gently explained I had other family commitments and suggested ways she might solve smaller problems on her own. I encouraged her to pray before making important decisions and assured her I would always be there for her. I reminded her that she could trust me and to always call for advice before making any big decisions.

She had lived fifty-five years on her own. But because of me she had become less self-reliant. Ruby had grown to trust herself less and trust me more to fix everything. It took me a while, but I finally admitted this to myself, and when I did, I could justify setting more boundaries.

I hoped she would understand.

NINETEEN

Quick to Judge

To help me with these boundaries, I asked Jesus to help Ruby make some more friends.

When Ruby pulled up to her apartment in a car instead of on her scooter, "friends" began appearing on her doorstep. Since that was not exactly what I meant, I amended my prayer to request, "friends she can trust."

She was in the infant stages of making friends, and I didn't want them to take advantage of her. I didn't want her to get hurt. Her willingness to trust was so fragile and new. Much like Ruby always warned me that I shouldn't go "pickin' up strangers," I didn't want her picking up strange friends.

I didn't always trust her judgment—think kittens and car repairmen—and I didn't know whether she could trust her neighbors or their motives. It seemed a little too coincidental that her popularity soared after she got a car.

I called her to ask her to go to lunch one Tuesday, since she'd not been calling as often. We hadn't seen one another for two weeks. The boundary talk was working, although I hoped not hurting.

"Can I bring a friend?" Ruby asked. "She lives here at the apartments."

"Of course, I'd love to meet your friend!" I answered enthusiastically. A friend for Ruby! I felt like a mom who picked her child up after her first day at a new school only to hear all about a friend she made.

"Where do you want to go? I asked, dreading the answer.

"Well, I'm low on gas, I've been drivin' folks to their appointments, so better meet close to here. You feel like the Chinese buffet?" she asked hopefully.

"Sure," I said with a grimace. "Why don't I just pick you both up and we can ride together. You're right on the way. How about 11:30 before they get too busy?" My stomach was already starting to roil just thinking of the buffet.

"I want her to meet you," Ruby said, "because when I been tellin' folks here about you, they don't believe I could have a friend like you. They seen you droppin' me off, and they said that nobody with a fancy car like yours would be my friend."

"Ruby, that makes me really upset. Did you tell her that I asked you to be my friend?" I didn't like being judged like this. "You didn't really want anything to do with me if you remember correctly."

I hoped I could be nice to this "friend," now that I had this information.

"I told her I knew you was my friend and that's all there is to it!" she said adamantly. Then her tone changed, and she asked, "You *are* my friend, right?"

My heart hurt that she still would ask me if I was her friend, and it hurt even worse for Ruby that someone would suggest I couldn't be her friend because of my car. How dare someone judge me because of the make of my vehicle! During the entire forty-five-minute drive to pick her up, I prayed for a supernatural grace toward her friend, to help me be friendly to her when we met.

When I arrived at the apartment complex to pick up Ruby, she was all dressed up in a new thrift store purchase: a sweatshirt with a cat pawing a ball of yarn on the front and some matching pink pants. She was wearing little pearl earrings (a dollar at Arch), and her hair was in a French braid. Her fingernails were long and polished bright pink. She looked amazing. This woman whose favorite creature was a butterfly had undergone her own transformation after spending many years in a cocoon.

We drove to another wing of the complex to pick up Ruby's friend. The woman was standing out front all dressed up too. Compared to the two of them, I was underdressed—just jeans and a flannel shirt. I didn't want to look fancy.

"Get in the back, Maria," Ruby said, adding, "This here's Cy, my friend."

"Hi, Maria, I am so glad to meet you. I haven't seen Ruby in a while, and I was missing her so much, I decided I had to drive up and have lunch with her." I made certain she knew this lunch was my idea.

"I'm just happy to finally meet you. Ruby talks about you all the time. She says you've been friends for a long time."

Actually, Maria seemed pretty sweet and sincere.

"About five years, I think. She didn't like me much when we first met, but I finally won her over, right Ruby?"

"I liked you fine. What are you talkin' about? I was just shy." Ruby wasn't working with me.

"Do you like Chinese food, Maria? It's Ruby's and my favorite. We especially love this buffet up on the corner."

As it turned out, in spite of the food, I had a really nice time. Maria was very kind and complimentary of Ruby, and I couldn't imagine that she had said those mean things to Ruby about our friendship.

Maria told me a bit of her tough life story. She was the single mother of a school-age son. She spoke of him lovingly and Ruby agreed he was a very well-mannered little boy. Maria and Ruby seemed to really enjoy one another's company. It was so interesting for me to watch Ruby interact with someone else besides my friends and family. She could be quite conversational and funny.

Maria needed to get home to meet her little boy after school, and when we dropped her off, I got out of the car and hugged her. She thanked me for the special afternoon and for the wonderful lunch. She argued with me briefly about paying for her lunch, but I told her I had a two-for-one coupon, so it was fine.

"Ruby," I said when I got back in the car, "Maria is so nice. I can't believe she would say that about my fancy car, and how I couldn't really be your friend!"

"Maria wasn't the one that said that." Ruby seemed surprised by my misunderstanding. "She told me about some other gal who don't even know me, saying it to her."

"Well, I am relieved to hear that. I was sitting there trying not to like her, but it wasn't working. I'm so happy you have such a nice friend."

I guess the person who was quick to judge turned out to be me.

"I got good judgement when it comes to friends. I picked you, didn't I?" she said with the impish smile I had come to know and love.

TWENTY

Barbed Wires Today, East Wing Tomorrow

Five years had passed since I'd attended Sam's first parole hearing with Ruby, and he was up for another hearing in December.

I started my letter writing campaign again. Bruce wrote letters, too. In our letters, we said that we would be his sponsors. We had no idea what that meant, but we would do it.

Through the years, we had grown closer to Sam through visitations. He sent us greeting cards carefully crafted from whatever scraps of paper he could get his hands on. He gave us each praying-hands belt buckles he'd made in metal shop when he was in Buena Vista. He made Whitney ceramic plaques of fairies and clowns. He wrote us beautiful letters. His faith in God grew. He asked for nothing but a Bible he could understand and some pens and paper so he could work on his art projects for Ruby. He was so soft spoken and polite. We understood why Ruby wanted to have him back in her life. She needed him. He needed her.

Ruby asked me to speak again at this hearing. I didn't want

to because I didn't feel I'd done very well at the previous one. I told her if she spoke, it might be more compelling. She said she would think about it, but she was still so angry. She wasn't sure she could keep her anger to herself.

Sterling was further than Buena Vista. On the day of the hearing, I drove to pick Ruby up. It was a cold winter morning when I arrived at her apartment at 4:30 a.m. *Really* cold. Despite the freezing temperatures, Ruby was out front smoking and waiting.

Ruby slept most of the way as I drove, and I woke her when we arrived at the prison. about 7:30. The maximum-security facility was so much starker and colder than the Buena Vista prison. Barbed wires, frozen ground, and gray, gray, gray was everywhere. I got shivers just looking at the facility. I turned up the heat in my car to eighty degrees as we pulled into the visitor parking area.

Ruby started to cry. I was teary, too. Neither one of us could bare to think of Sam living here. Stabbings were frequent at this horrible cement container for criminals. I wanted bad guys to be in there. I just didn't believe Ruby's brother was a bad guy.

If I thought it had been difficult getting into Buena Vista, that was nothing compared to this experience. I was scared. I was filled with such apprehension I could barely breathe as we went through a series of barred gates that clanged shut behind us each time we walked through one. The prison was much larger but felt far more claustrophobic. It felt like a tomb—maybe because people *had* died within these walls.

We were escorted to a room with other waiting visitors. The anxiety was palpable.

"I ain't speakin'," Ruby said, breaking the uneasy silence.

I had been expecting this, but I still asked her why.

"They don't care what I say. They ain't gonna ever let him out."

"Do you want me to speak, then?" I asked Ruby. But I really didn't need to. Who else was there?

A guard walked into the room and read from a clipboard: "Family of prisoner number 4415."

"That's us," I said in a small voice to Ruby. We stood and followed the guard.

The parole board was waiting for us. Sam was wearing a jump suit and shackles and stood next to one of the guards. As we entered the room, Sam looked up at Ruby and smiled. He said hi to me. Ruby didn't reach out to touch him like the last time. Lesson learned.

"Ruby, if you'd like to hug your brother, go ahead," one of the parole board members said. "After all, you came all this way to see him."

Surprised, Ruby said thank you and hugged her brother hard.

"Thanks, Sis," Sam said. "I love you. Don't cry."

One of the board members announced that the proceedings were being recorded. Someone else on the board introduced all of our names into the record and welcomed us. Then he read a document describing the crime for which Sam had already served twenty-four years. The document included vivid details. I had never heard the details told so graphically, and I felt a bit faint. Ruby continued to silently weep while her brother, hands behind his back, went back to staring at the floor.

Then the parole board member turned to me. "Were you aware of the violence of this crime, Mrs. DeBoer?"

"No."

"I understand you would like to speak on the inmate's behalf."

"Yes, I would. The man who was convicted of that crime is not the man I know. He, along with his sister, have become dear friends of our family."

"How do you know each other? Did you know him or his sister before his incarceration? How has he changed, in your opinion?"

I tried to explain the story of Ruby's and my friendship, how it began and how it had grown. I explained her many health issues. I talked about the positive impact his release would have on both of their lives. I told them of my husband's and my commitment to be a support system for both of them, particularly for her brother as he got back on his feet. I spoke of our standing in the community and gave as many reasons as I could possibly muster why he should be paroled. I was able to say more than I had at the last hearing.

"Thank you, Mrs. DeBoer," one of the board members said. "You've been a good friend to Ruby, and she is lucky to have you and your husband."

And with that, my time was done.

The board members continued to ask Sam about his remorsefulness, and he could only say he had no memory of the crime but was very sad for the family.

"I want to help my sister She ain't well. Please let me take care of her," he said tearfully.

When it was over, we were granted permission to hug him and say goodbye. Then we were escorted from the room.

Ruby and I headed back through the clanging gates. Back to the car. Back to Ruby's apartment. Ruby slept most of the way home. She looked much older than when we had started out that morning. The butterfly had gone back in her cocoon.

Twenty-four hours later I found myself standing behind a red velvet rope at the East Wing of the White House instead of the black iron bars of the previous day. Our son, had arranged for Bruce and me to get a private tour of the White House Christmas decorations.

It was a beautiful sight, but my heart was still behind bars.

Parole had not been granted.

TWENTY-ONE

God Chose the Street

In the spring, Bruce and I were on one of those purposeless Sunday drives when we made a spur-of-the-moment decision to visit an open house in a neighborhood we'd always loved. Castle Pines Village was ten miles south of where we lived and filled with beautiful lodge pole pines scrub oak, and winding roads. The Village was also home to abundant wildlife such as deer, elk and wild turkeys.

So when we saw the open house signs, we couldn't resist.

We weren't looking for a bigger house. In fact, with our son, Ryan, working in Washington and our daughter starting her sophomore year in college, we were on the verge of becoming empty nesters. I'm pretty sure Bruce had thought of downsizing, but for crying out loud, I'm not a mind reader.

As we toured the house, we liked it but not enough to get excited about it. Tom, the developer, happened to be the one showing the house and he thought for a moment then said, "I have one house you might be interested in. It is a bit higher in price than this one. We have it framed and most of the drywall hung. Would you like to see it? It's just up the hill."

Bruce and I answered at the same time.

"No thanks, we aren't really looking," Bruce said.

"Yes!" I cried.

Tom apparently had selective hearing and wisely selected to hear me.

We followed him up the hill to the house under construction.

We walked through the front door, and I felt I had just entered the perfect home. Every corner I turned drew me in further. Each floor to ceiling window revealed majestic hundred-year-old pine trees peeking in from every direction.

From the circular driveway, the house looked like a charming one-story chalet; its size was all in the back of the house. It was a house that said, "Welcome to Colorado."

I wandered around for forty-five minutes, circling back to each room several times. I could tell Bruce liked it also. He is usually pretty quick to point out design or structure flaws, but I didn't hear a single disparaging remark.

It was bigger than we needed, that is, *if* we were thinking of buying, which we were not. We lay in bed that night talking about everything but the house.

Until we started talking about the house.

"It's too big, really," Bruce said.

"True, but we'd only live on the main floor, and our kids and overnight guests would have the amazing lower level to themselves," I countered.

"It has a great lot," Bruce said thoughtfully.

"It *does* have a great lot." I agreed.

"I like the location." Bruce accidentally confessed.

"I *love* the location." After a moment of silence, I added, "Might be able to put in a putting green." I had stopped playing fair.

"Well, we can talk more about it tomorrow. Good night."

"Night."

We made an offer. It was accepted. We chose all the interior colors, light fixtures, flooring and finishes.

But God chose the street name: We hadn't even noticed the street sign: Ruby Trust Court.

TWENTY-TWO

Heaven Scent Christmas

"*J* still can't believe you got them to name your street after me!" Ruby said gleefully.

She had just pulled into our driveway, and I was helping her out of the car.

"Every time I turn that corner," she added, "it makes me so happy."

"It is pretty amazing. It makes me smile, too," I agreed, laughing. I never had the heart to tell her the street was already named when we bought the house.

Ryan had just come out from the house to greet Ruby. He was home for Christmas from DC along with his girlfriend, Courtney. Ruby was wearing a bright red sweatshirt with blue snowmen and white snowflakes. Her nails were painted bright Ruby red!

"Hi Ruby. You look very festive," Ryan said.

"Hi, Bryan, I got some things in the back of the car I could use your help with."

Ryan hugged her, not bothering to remind her his name was not Bryan. "What is all of this? Looks like a lot of presents."

"Ain't much, but I found a few things at Arch on sale. My brother sent some things too."

"Let's get inside, it's cold," I said.

"Hey, Ruby!" Bruce met her at the front door with a bear hug. "Welcome and merry Christmas. I'm glad you could join us."

Ruby stood with her arms to her side during the hugs. Hugging still made her uncomfortable.

Standing next to Bruce, Whitney's greeted Ruby. "Ruby, hi, merry Christmas!"

Inside the house, Bruce's mom was in a chair by the window, and Ruby was quick to sit in the chair next to Grandma. They both liked to park themselves and let the rest of us buzz all around them. After hosting holiday dinners for more than thirty years, I can totally see myself in the future finding a comfortable chair and not moving until the dinner bell rings or nature calls.

One of the things I love about entertaining is setting the table. I'm all about the ambience, and I love to keep the lights low, the candles lit, and the table festive.

Cooking? Not so much.

For years, I ordered meals from delicatessens and restaurants, quickly transferring food from the disposable foil pans to my own dishes (then hiding the pans and boxes). I even wore an apron, which I broke out twice a year. Of course, all of my clandestine activity was a waste of time because as soon as we sat down to dinner and people began complimenting me on the various culinary delights, I would blurt, "Oh, I didn't make that. You can order it from Tony's." This always drove my husband crazy as he felt I should take credit for the whole thing since I had worked hard ordering, decorating, and planning for days. But to tell a lie on Jesus's birthday just doesn't seem right.

Besides, what if someone wanted the recipe? I just couldn't do it. (I do, however, make my own gravy. In fact, I am the queen of gravy! I can clog arteries with the best of them!)

Ruby loves to eat. We had her over almost every holiday dinner, so she arrived with her own set of expectations. And she voiced them as we were approaching the table to say grace.

"You got them croissants this year?" she asked, practically smacking her lips. "I love them things. Is that real butter or margarine? Have any jelly?"

"Ruby," I said, laughing, "you're down here at the end with me. Yep, we have croissants and it is real butter. I'll check on the jelly."

It dawned on me that she probably had some in her handbag.

We all stood behind our chairs while Bruce said grace, thoughtfully remembering all those who weren't with us, and acknowledging that Jesus was the reason any of us were there at all. Then we all proceeded to the buffet.

Ryan and Whitney filled Grandma's and Ruby's plates so they could stay comfortably seated at the table. It seemed altruistic, but it was actually a strategic move to keep the buffet line moving. Ruby had a tendency to congest the line. I'd seen her at the Chinese buffet pondering each choice as though it were life-or-death decision.

After we were seated and sated, the entertainment portion of the meal commenced. Ryan and Whitney knew the drill and exchanged their "here goes Mom again" look and rolled their eyes. I fantasize that someday this tradition will be carried on, with Ryan and Whitney posing similar questions to *their* families, and their children will exchange the same looks and eye rolls. After all, every Thanksgiving Bruce asks everyone to share something they were grateful for. Every Christmas, I gave a different suggestion. "Please say something you especially appreciate about the person on your right," I said, explaining my simple idea for that year.

.

Ruby didn't love this part of the dining experience either. But she was a good sport. I was careful to seat her between Whitney and me. I knew she would be comfortable praising Whitney, and I would have the opportunity, since she was to my right, of sharing how much I appreciated her. Whether she liked it or not, she stole the show with her heartfelt words of appreciation. She didn't stop with Whitney; she went around the table and spoke to each of us. She reminded us all of the joy that comes from sharing. We all felt more appreciative of our blessings when we were able to share them with Ruby. Christmas with Ruby on Ruby Trust Court was totally arranged by Jesus, and we all knew it.

After we went around the table hearing everyone's answers, we finished up with confetti party poppers. It's an English tradition we follow because we think it's fun, not because we are English. We grip our poppers on each end and tug at the count of three. Paper crowns, some "Cracker Jack" style trinkets, and a few slips of paper with jokes and riddles explode out of the middle. We put on our crowns and take turns reading our corny riddles aloud.

Ruby announced that we were weird, but both she and Grandma wore their crowns for the remainder of the day.

After dinner, we gathered around the Christmas tree. Bruce, Ryan, Whitney, and I had opened our gifts to each other that morning, and the gifts that were left had been moved to another room to make way for a dessert party later in the evening. Still under the tree, however, were our gifts to Ruby, and the packages we had brought in from her car.

Her beautiful, humble presents were wrapped in newspaper, from the front pages to the funnies, and each had a random-colored bow stuck on it. All of our color-coordinated packages paled in comparison.

Ruby meticulously unwrapped each of her gifts, trying to not tear the paper, which she folded neatly before opening the box. She seemed happy with whatever she found inside, exclaiming every time, "I ain't never had nothing so nice before!"

She handed each of us—Bruce, Whitney, and me—two gifts, one from her and one from her brother. She apologized to Ryan and Courtney for not having anything for them because "I didn't know you was going to be here." Both graciously thanked her for the gift of spending Christmas with us.

Bruce opened his gift from Sam first. "Wow! This is amazing!" he exclaimed. "Did he make this?" He held up an eighteen-inch-tall pottery beer stein. It was hand-painted in a German theme.

"He made it a while back when he was able to do his crafts," Ruby said proudly. "He hopes you like beer."

"I love it, please tell him how nice it was of him to think of me. I can't wait to use it." Bruce was genuinely amazed by the thoughtfulness of the gift. It was big enough to hold a six pack!

Then he picked up his second present. "Let's see what I have here from Ruby," he said, carefully pulling the comics away from his gift. It was a pocket-sized address book.

"It ain't much," Ruby said apologetically, "but I figured you can use something to keep track of whatever it is you do."

"It's perfect. Mine will be expiring in a few days when we start the new year. Great timing!"

His words made Ruby smile.

"My turn?" Whit was already opening her gift from Ruby's

brother. "Awesome! I can't believe he made this!" She held up a ceramic figure of a half-moon with a fairy sitting in the curve of the moon.

"He figured you might like that to decorate your room," Ruby explained. "He wasn't for sure what you liked."

"This is perfect. And the fairy's dress is blue, my favorite color," Whitney said. I smiled at her wonderful grace. Her bedroom was nothing but hockey posters and framed jerseys, and her college dorm room had no wall space for a fairy on a moon. But she told Ruby it was the best gift of the day. It definitely was the most meaningful.

"And Ruby, thank you for these earrings! They are so pretty!" Whitney had opened her present from Ruby and was already removing her own earrings to replace them with the little silver hearts Ruby had given her. Whitney looked again at the newspaper wrappings and exclaimed, "No way, a matching ring?"

"I got 'em from a lady at my apartment who used to sell Avon. She showed me these, and I thought they looked like you. You have a big heart, Whitney. The ring is adjustable, so I hope it fits. That red velvet box came with it." Ruby seemed really pleased with her gift for Whitney.

"Cy, your turn." Bruce pointed out.

I carefully un-taped the newspaper to reveal my present from Ruby's brother. It was a ten-inch-square mirror featuring a painted image of blue praying hands surrounded by red hearts. Like Bruce's beer stein, and Whitney's fairy moon, my mirror had been hand-painted with love. With tears in my eyes, I told Ruby, "Your brother is so talented and thoughtful. I can't believe he made us each such perfect gifts."

"He loves yer family. He says he prays for you every night. He still can't believe all ya'll do for us. He loved that package of food you sent 'em. I hope he ain't eatin' it all at once and gettin' himself sick. He hates that prison food, so he's pretty hungry most of the time."

I opened my gift from Ruby.

"Ruby, how did you know this was the dusting powder my mother and grandmother both used? Heaven Scent!"

I didn't even know they made dusting powder with the big fluffy puffs anymore. I imagine ARC had this round blue pearlized container sitting on a shelf just waiting for Ruby to buy it and give it to me for Christmas. It was truly Heaven sent, just like Ruby. I jumped out of my chair and gave Ruby a giant hug. I knew I could get away with it because she was sitting deep in an overstuffed chair and couldn't escape.

We cleaned up round two of the gift opening and got ready for the next onslaught of guests. Every year, we host Bruce's side of the family for dessert. About twenty-four guests (mostly kids) arrive around 6:30 as we are putting the last dinner dish in the dishwasher. (Whenever Ryan is with us, this task goes much more quickly. He is a master at loading a dishwasher.)

Courtney, Whitney, and I began unboxing desserts and whipping the cream. (I break my spray canned cream habit only for Christmas). We set out more plates, forks, and spoons. As guests began to arrive, Bruce took coats and drink orders. We functioned like a well-oiled machine—as we should, after doing it for so many years.

I could tell Ruby was tired and wanted to desert, but not before dessert. She eyed the dining table laden with pumpkin and pecan pies, ice cream, cookies, brownies, divinity, fudge, and other sugary offerings brought by our relatives. The sweet spread held her attention for a bit longer.

The highlight of the dessert tradition was Whitney's birthday cake for Jesus. She has been decorating a cake for Jesus every year since she was three years old. She was working with apprentice younger cousins, so we can keep the tradition alive.

We turned out all the lights and lit the candles on Jesus's cake. Honoring the most important birthday of the year, we sang "Happy Birthday" to Jesus. I reveled in the fact that it had been a glorious (and exhausting!) celebration in every way.

A few hours later as Bruce and I nestled down in our bed, I won't lie, visions of Christmas in Hawaii danced in our heads.

TWENTY-THREE

U-Haul and Then U-Haul Some More

Ruby's brother was moved from Sterling Prison to Canon City State Prison, again, with no notice or explanation. It was painful for him because he had begun his prison term in Canon City over a quarter century before.

Thankfully, he was only there for a few months before being sent to a minimum-security facility near Canon City. This was good news. In the minimum-security facility he would have more freedom to be outside and work around the prison. He could also do more of his crafts.

Shortly after Sam's transfer, I got a call from Ruby.

"I found me a trailer," she announced. "I'm movin' closer to my brother."

"What? When?" I asked, surprised, even though it had been getting more difficult for her to shock me.

Ruby had talked before about getting a little trailer for Lizzie Lou and the cats somewhere in the mountains. She'd been dreaming of a little yard and some peace and quiet. She'd long envisioned having a trailer out in the middle of nowhere, not in a trailer park

"Where is the trailer? Have you seen it? Does the owner take Section 8?" I asked.

"I been talkin' to the owner. He says he takes Section 8. It's in a trailer court in Florence. It's just a few miles from where my brother is. I'll be able to see him more. The long drive is hard on me, and I can't afford the gas. I can move in next week. I drove by the trailer park last time I went to see my brother. I ain't got no idea which trailer, but the place didn't look so bad."

"What about your doctors?" I pressed, worried now. "What about me? I won't be able to see you as often, or be close enough to help if you need me."

"They got hospitals and doctors down there. I'll miss you, but you are so busy. And you ain't got a real need for me; my bother does. Besides, you can come visit me or we can meet up in Colorado Springs."

I nodded, still in shock.

She continued. "I ain't happy at that apartment no more anyway. There's been some rough people movin' in. I think there's lots of drugs. It ain't like it was when I got there. Maria's gone, and since she passed, I am sad being there and thinkin' of her all the time. I got me some good friends there, but they are always needing rides and help. I just ain't got the money or strength to keep up."

"This seems so sudden, Ruby." I was apprehensive. "Have you given notice at your apartment? How are you going to move your things?"

"I gave 'em notice a couple of weeks ago. I'm gettin' a little of my deposit back."

I wasn't surprised she wasn't getting the whole thing back. Lizzie Lou and Kitty Cats 1 and 2 had left their marks, literally. (Kitty Cat 3 was killed when poor Ruby accidentally rocked back in her recliner, and he was caught in it.)

Oh my gosh, Lord, I don't like this at all. Is this your idea?

Ruby cleared her throat. "So I was wonderin' if after I was all loaded up I could come by your house, and you could follow me down to the trailer and help me get set up. I want you to see the place, and I'd feel better drivin' the truck if you was followin' me."

"I could probably work that out, but Ruby with my one hand that is almost useless and my not so stellar back, I don't think I could be much help moving and lifting. Bruce works all week and I don't know anyone who could help us in Florence."

"A few of them fellas around the apartment said since I was givin' them some of my furniture, they'd help me load the rest in a U-Haul. So, I'll have me some deposit money to use for the U-Haul"

I nodded again and felt a lump in my throat.

"That ol' boy I'm rentin' from owns a few of the trailers in that park and said if I was to call him about an hour before I show up, he knows a couple of fellas that can move me in. They'll want some money. He didn't give me no idea how much. I'm gonna pay you back for everything, I promise. I feel bad always askin' you to help. I just don't know what else to do."

I knew it was always hard on her to ask. And it was impossible for me to say no.

Clearly, Ruby already had lots of wheels in motion, but, of course, there were a few things she hadn't considered. She needed more money to rent the truck, deposit for the trailer, and first and last month's rent.

Plan B came to the rescue again.

A few days later, a sixteen-foot U-Haul truck pulled up in front of our house with Ruby's Taurus wagon hitched behind. Apparently, they didn't have a smaller truck available. Her car would have fit in the truck, because her things, stacked loosely, only filled about a fourth of it. Ruby looked like a ten-year-old with gray braids driving that huge truck.

When I saw her, I said, "Hey there, Edith Ann." She didn't get the Carol Burnett reference.

She was sitting on pillows and I have no idea how her feet reached the gas and brakes. Lizzie Lou was in the front seat, and the two cats were in a kennel on the floor of the cab.

"Ruby, couldn't you get a bigger truck?" I tried a second stab at a little humor.

"Nah, this is the biggest they got."

I was never sure if she knew when I was joking.

"Okay," I sighed. "Well, let's head out. Need anything? Water? Snacks?"

"Nah, I got all I need."

"Okay, let's hit the road."

Oh, the places she takes me, the places we go, I thought.

Traveling at forty-five miles per hour for about one hundred miles (and a couple of cigarette breaks) put us at the dirt lot of her new home in about five hours. I had been eager to arrive. It was awful. The U-Haul was bigger than Ruby's new home.

When we called the manager, he said he'd head right over with some help.

We waited. And waited some more. Eventually we took a scary walk with Lizzie Lou past a neighbor's wolf dog tied to a stake. The wolf dog barked and pulled hard at his rope. Lizzie Lou barked back, still oblivious to her diminutive stature.

After half an hour, the landlord pulled up with a couple of rough-looking characters. We made our introductions and the trailer door was unlocked for our inspection.

It felt like Ruby and I had been cast in a B horror movie. The inside of the trailer was musty. Two cracked windows were repaired with peeling duct tape, through which the wind whistled eerily. The door rattled in unison with the whistling. Neither the refrigerator or stove looked like they worked. I feared if I opened the refrigerator door, I might find body parts.

I pointed out the problems to the landlord. Oh, how I longed to point out something good about the place, but nothing was jumping out at me other than my nerves.

While the seedy characters unloaded the truck, I pulled Ruby aside and shared my very serious concerns.

"Ruby, is this what you were expecting? Do you feel comfortable staying here? Because we can go back to my house and think this over." If she liked the place, I didn't want to hurt her feelings, since she had found it on her own, At the same time, I expected to hear a chainsaw starting up any minute.

"Nah, it ain't that bad. I been in worse. He said he'd fix them windows and lock. I ain't fond of that dog next door. I hope Lizzie will be alright." Overall, Ruby was far less freaked-out than me.

The guys turned the refrigerator on, proved the stove worked, and moved the furniture in. I had grown to like them. They thanked me for the money and told Ruby to let them know if she ever needed anything else. One of them gave her a business card.

We had just enough time to return the U-Haul to a facility in Canon City before the rental place closed. On the way back we stopped at a Safeway to pick up a few things to put in Ruby's mini refrigerator and micro-mini cupboards. I felt bad because I had to leave before helping her unload any boxes, but I needed to get back home before dark or Bruce would be worried. I'm not sure I ever told him the nitty-gritty of the day's adventure.

Six months later, we loaded Ruby's things into a U-Haul

and moved her back north. Being close to her brother was great, but the living conditions that winter had been hard. Her car didn't do well in the snow, and the trailer never got warm. She was constantly coughing and becoming more depressed. Living in the trailer park had been lonelier than living in her apartment and, she missed our family more than she thought she would.

We had to get Section 8 Housing approval in a new county and start the process of setting up another place for Ruby. I was beginning to learn the ropes. The new apartment in Arapahoe County was a nice two-bedroom unit, much closer to our house. She hoped that the second bedroom would belong to her brother someday.

The State had changed the interval between parole hearings from five years to three years, and Sam was up for another shot at parole. Bruce joined me this time. I thought his distinguished presence might be compelling, lending credence to our pledge to help him after parole.

During the hearing, Bruce spoke of the man he knew and had come to genuinely care about. He said it was his impression that prison was supposed to help rehabilitate, not stifle, and that he hoped a prisoner's pattern of good behavior would be taken into consideration during these hearings. At that point Sam had served twenty-eight years.

This time, Sam even had a second person vouch for him. A prison guard took unpaid time off to speak up for Ruby's brother. The guard said Sam was the guy they went to for everything. He did all the repairs around the prison—even in the middle of the night. He was one of the "good guys," the guard said, adding that he had never spoken on behalf of a prisoner before.

He actually said Sam would truly be missed when he was paroled.

Again, parole was denied.

TWENTY-FOUR

Lizzie Lou

"Hi, Ruby, what's up?" My morning wake-up call was a little later than usual. "Ruby, are you there? Ruby? We must have a bad connection."

"I'm here."

I'd never heard Ruby cry out loud. I'd seen tears but never heard such sobbing and despair.

"Lizzie Lou is dead."

"Oh, Ruby, I am so, so sorry. What happened?"

She just kept crying.

"I'm coming over, Ruby. I'm leaving now."

"I ain't home. I'm at the vet's," she managed to say. "They put her down; she was real sick. She musta had cancer." She choked out the words.

"Wasn't this sudden?" I was surprised by the news. "You never told me she wasn't doing alright."

"I been noticing she was slowing down. She's sixteen. She ain't been eatin' real good. Safeway's been out of the salmon flavor food she likes, so I thought maybe she was mad about not havin' her favorite flavor. I shoulda gone to another store to get the salmon." The guilt in her voice was apparent. "She was vomiting blood this morning, so I ran her over to the vet's office."

"Ruby, you have loved Lizzie Lou and cared for her even when you could barely feed yourself. Gosh, I had no idea she was that old. You've been such an amazing friend to her," I consoled. "Can I meet you at the vet?"

"Nah, I want to sit here with her awhile. Just the two of us. We was always just the two of us, and I want to be alone with her. The doctor said I could stay as long as I want. Don't worry, Cy, I'll be alright. I just wanted to let you know. Would you tell Whitney? I know you both loved her."

What a way to pour on the guilt. I didn't exactly *love* Lizzie Lou, but I'd certainly loved what she meant to Ruby.

"Ruby, if you change your mind, call me. Are you alright to drive?"

"I'll be fine. Thank you, Cy, I love you."

"I love you, too, Ruby. Why don't you ask the veterinarian if he can make you a memorial paw print in cement for you? Have him send me the bill for everything from today. It would make us feel good to know we helped with her final expenses. Will you do that for me?"

She agreed, and I hung up feeling helplessly sad for my friend.

Ruby mourned Lizzie Lou every day for weeks. Her most trusted friend of sixteen years was gone, leaving anther dent in Ruby's battered heart.

The era of Ruby and Layla began three months later when Layla, a vagrant Chihuahua, turned up on Ruby's doorstep. Actually, a neighbor showed up with Layla on a leash, since he was moving to an apartment where he couldn't have a dog.

And just like that, Layla stepped into Lizzie Lou's paws, and the silence that had fallen over Ruby's apartment came to an end.

Layla, like Lizzie Lou, was infatuated with the sound of her own bark. Unlike her predecessor, however, Layla liked people. Petting her didn't seem dangerous. Layla and Kitty Cats 1 and 2 raced through the apartment until it was impossible to determine who was chasing whom.

Layla was drawn to the same space at the foot of Ruby's bed that had once belonged to Lizzie Lou. Layla fit perfectly in the depression Lizzie Lou left on the comforter, and the hollow spot in Ruby's heart.

TWENTY-FIVE

Twenty-Four Hours

"May I speak with Cy DeBoer?" the voice on the other end asked.

"Yes, may I ask who is calling?'

"My name is Shirley. I work at a rest stop between Castle Rock and Colorado Springs. There was a lady in here using the restroom, and she passed out on the floor. We called an ambulance. When they were loading her up, she gave the driver your number, and he gave it to me to call you."

"Where is the ambulance taking her?" I asked frantically.

"They said Sky Ridge Medical Center in Lone Tree." Shirley sounded shaken. "Her car is parked here. We will keep an eye on it until someone can come get it. I hope she's alright."

"Thank you, Shirley. I appreciate your call and your kindness. I will let you know when I can get the car."

I was about to hang up when Shirley added, "She looked really, really bad. I'd get to the hospital soon if I was you."

Fortunately, the hospital was just a few miles away from our house. I rushed over there, and by the time I found her, she was already being prepped for surgery.

"Please," I pleaded with a nurse at the door leading to the operating room. "I need to see her if she hasn't already gone to surgery. She won't do well if I can't talk to her for a minute. Is she conscious? I just need to see her. Can you go back and talk to someone?"

"Let me check for you," the nurse said. "I believe she is still in pre-op. Are you family?"

"Yes. Please hurry."

In a few minutes another nurse came through the automatic door, looked at me, and asked, "Are you Cy?"

"Yes, where is Ruby?"

"Thank goodness you're here. She won't consent to surgery without you. She says you are her next of kin and power of attorney."

"I am."

Thankfully, with Bruce being a lawyer and Ruby having so many health issues, her doctors had recommended a living will for Ruby and she made me power of attorney.

When I entered the room, the surgeon and anesthesiologist were talking to Ruby, who seemed to be disagreeing with everything they were saying.

As soon as Ruby saw me, she cried out, "Cy, you found me! I told them they wasn't doing nothin' to me until they explained it to you first. I also gotta talk to my brother."

A stern and impatient surgeon shook my hand quickly. "It is truly life or death, Mrs. DeBoer. She will most likely wake up with an ostomy bag and need a great deal of medical care for an extended period of time. She is septic, her blood pressure is very high, and her chances are very slim, unless she consents to this surgery. She is being very difficult and, frankly, she is running out of time. She says she has a brother in prison she also needs to consult with. There isn't time for any such thing."

Thanks for sugar-coating it, Dr. Bedside Manner. No wonder she's scared.

"Thank you, Doctor," I said politely. "I will just need a minute to speak with her alone."

The doctor gave the nurse orders to come back in in exactly one minute to get the signed release.

As soon as they left, I turned to Ruby.

"Ruby, you are very ill. You need this surgery. I will be here waiting for you when you come out of the operating room."

"What if I die? I want to tell my brother I love him. I want him to never give up." She was near hysterics. "Promise me you will help him get on his feet if he ever gets out?"

"I promise, Ruby. My family will be here for both of you. Let's pray together right now and get you off to surgery." I knew the clock was ticking.

We held hands.

"Lord, Jesus, please hold Ruby's hand and guide the surgeon and the team taking care of her in the operating room. Take away her fear and calm her with your presence. Lord, you know how much I love Ruby, and I know how much You love Ruby. Let her go off to sleep in the confidence that You will never leave her side."

I opened the door and asked the nurse to come back in. Ruby was ready to sign the form.

"Ruby," said the sweet nurse, "if I were going to have this surgery, I would pick your surgeon. He may seem a little grouchy, but believe me, he is the best. I work with him in the OR all the time. He will take very good care of you. I promise."

Ruby signed the forms with her beautiful handwriting, even with an IV in the top of her hand, and then the nurses rolled her away.

Our nurse came back to get something from the room as I was just leaving.

"I understand you have zero time," I said, "but quickly I have to tell you something important." I gave her a sixty-second rundown of our story. I told her how much I loved Ruby and informed her about her brother in prison and their love for each other. I begged her to tell the doctor Ruby's story and, not that I doubted he wouldn't, to ask him to take very good care of her.

She wiped tears from her eyes, hugged me, and promised she would relay the story and my love for Ruby to the doctor.

I called Whitney because I thought she might be out of class and wanted her company. She arrived a half hour later to sit with me in the waiting room. I also called Bruce and he joined us after work. When I called Ryan, who was working in Vail, he said he would pray for Ruby and asked me to keep him posted.

I called Sam's case manager at the prison. The sergeant who answered the phone told me the case manager was gone for the day and asked if he could redirect my call.

I gave him my name and Ruby's brother's name.

"Sure, I know him. He's a good guy, does a lot of work around here."

I was relieved the sergeant actually knew him.

"I need to get a message to him. His sister is undergoing a life-threatening surgery right now. There is a very good chance she won't live, and if I need to call him with that news, I would like someone to be with him. Does the prison have a chaplain?"

"I'm really sorry to hear about Sam's sister." He seemed genuinely concerned. "Let me see what I can find out about the chaplain. Can I take your number and call you back?"

While we waited, Whitney and I shared Ruby stories and tried to fill the hours that were oh so slowly ticking by. We read magazines. We exhausted our sugar limits at the vending machines. She did homework. I paced like a caged lion.

After what felt like days, the desk attendant made an announcement. "Is someone here with Ruby Jean?"

"We are!" Whitney and I spoke in unison.

"I have an operating nurse on the phone to speak with you," she said and pointed us to a phone.

I answered with my heart in my throat. "Hello, this is Cy."

"Hi, Cy, it's Julie. We spoke as Ruby left for surgery."

"Yes, hello. How is she doing?"

"I am calling because the doctor would like you to get in touch with her brother. I am very sorry. We almost lost her a couple of times, and he may need to sew her up soon. He would like to bring Ruby around enough to give her a few minutes to talk to her brother and say goodbye. Do you think there is any chance you could make that happen?"

"Oh, my Lord, of course, I will do everything I can. I will make some calls right now. Thank you." I was crying.

"We aren't there yet," she said, trying to console me, "but we want you to start working on it as soon as possible."

I called the sergeant back and explained the dire state of affairs.

"I reached the chaplain. He was heading home, about an hour away. But based on what you told me, he's already turned around and is coming back. He likes Sam a lot. He always comes to the chapel when he's not working around the prison." The sergeant's voice was kind. "The minute he gets here I'll have him get Sam on the phone."

"Bless you. I'll wait for his call."

"I'm praying for his sister," he added kindly.

Bruce arrived and the three of us prayed, cried, paced, and waited. We anxiously wondered what would come first, the call from the operating room or the call from the chaplain and Ruby's brother?

Before long, the hospital chaplain arrived. She offered to call the prison if we thought that would help, and she said she could sit with us, too. We thanked her and assured her we would let her know if we needed her to make any calls. In the meantime, it was six in the evening, and we figured it was time for her to head home to her family. We had her cell number.

Just then my phone rang.

It was the prison chaplain.

"I have Ruby's brother beside me to speak with you about Ruby," he said gently.

"Hi, Cy. What's happening to Ruby?" Sam asked in a shaky voice.

"I'm sorry, but she is not doing well. She is in surgery. I haven't heard from the nurse in over an hour, but last we spoke, at the suggestion of the surgeon, she asked me to let you know the situation is very grim."

I could hear him quietly weeping on the other end of the line. It took a minute for him to compose himself enough to continue speaking.

"Is my sister going to die? God, please tell me she isn't going to die. This life has been so hard on her because of me. I should be with her. I've done this to her." He was broken to the bone. It was the deepest sorrow I had ever heard. "The chaplain said something about talking to her on the phone. Can I please talk to her, please?"

"She is still in surgery and I am waiting to hear from the operating room nurse as to whether she will be awake enough to talk. Wait a few moments. Bruce is going to ask the waiting room attendant to call the operating room and let them know you are on the phone. Let's pray together, Sam. Maybe the chaplain can lead us."

While the prison chaplain said a beautiful calming prayer, Bruce stood waiting for an answer from the volunteer at the desk.

When Bruce returned, he said, "They said there is no one available to talk right now. They are sorry. It may be awhile before we hear anything else."

I relayed the message to Sam.

"Can I speak with the chaplain for a moment?" I asked her brother.

He took the phone off speaker, and I said, "I appreciate your help so much. I don't want her brother to be alone, but I realize you have family and were on your way home. It sounds like it could be a long wait before we know anything more. Do you have any suggestions on how to best comfort him, while we wait?"

"I do have to be home in a while, the best I can offer is to have the sergeant you spoke with, who has offered his help, keep checking on him through the night. It will be lockdown soon, but he said he will still keep an eye on him since he is the night duty officer. I will leave you my cell number, and you can call me if you need to get a hold of her brother with news. Still, I don't think he will be able to talk to her if she wakes up tonight. I wish I could do more," he added sincerely.

"You have been a great help, thank you. I will let you know when I hear anything. Good night."

"You are all in my prayers. Thank you for all you've done. Sam speaks very highly of your family. He's a good man. Good night."

About two hours later, the nurse called me on my cell phone. "Are you still here at the hospital?" she asked.

"I am. How is Ruby?" I asked, knowing the answer and trying to hold it together.

"She is in recovery; the doctor will be out to talk to you in a few minutes. I just wanted you to know she is still alive," she reported cautiously and then hung up.

AN EXHAUSTED MAN wearing scrubs and a blue surgical mask around his neck approached the circle of leather chairs where we sat waiting. No one else was in the room.

We stood to greet him.

"Ruby is alive," the doctor said. "If she makes it through the night that will tell us a lot about whether the surgery was successful. During the procedure, I was able to visually conference with my colleague who was finishing a surgery in our sister hospital across town. He recently had a similarly complicated surgery with a patient who was younger and in better physical health than Ruby. However, he was able to perform a resection of the diseased bowel and intestines without removing the colon. We decided it was Ruby's best chance of survival to try the same procedure."

Standing between Whitney and Bruce, the three of us were holding hands. "So she is going to live?" I half asked and half exclaimed. I felt exhausted, but in a state of cautious euphoria. Then I cried out, "I need to call her brother!"

"I wouldn't do that just yet," the doctor spoke. "Ruby has a lot of factors working against her. She has very poor arteries, high blood pressure, weak heart tissue, and her lungs are in terrible shape from so many years of smoking. She still has a long road ahead of her. She needs to make it at least twenty-four hours out of surgery before we can get too hopeful. She will be heading to intensive care, and you will not be able to see her tonight. You all need to go home and get some rest," he added kindly. This didn't seem at all like the surgeon I met over nine hours ago in pre-op.

I realized I hadn't introduced anyone. "Doctor, this is my husband, Bruce and our daughter, Whitney. They've been here with me waiting."

"Nice to meet you both. Whitney, are you in school at Denver University?" he asked, noticing her DU sweatshirt, then added, "It's a good school."

"I am. Thank you for saving Ruby. We love her, she is part of our family," Whitney said, wiping away tears.

"I heard something to that affect from a surgical nurse just before surgery. And Ruby certainly loves all of you." He slightly smiled and gave me a conspiratorial wink.

Lord, bless that wonderful nurse. She was our voice when we were unable to speak.

My heart was filled with gratitude.

Thank you, Jesus, for putting that nurse in Ruby's life. Thank you for this gifted surgeon and others who used the skills you gave them to do their very best to save Ruby.

THE NEXT MORNING as Bruce and I were signing our names for admittance to the ICU, we heard a voice behind us.

"Good morning. You're here early."

We turned. It was the doctor.

"Doctor! Look who's talking. How is she? I checked with the desk all through the night and they said she was holding her own."

"She is indeed. She is holding a court of nurses and asking when she can go home." He actually broke into a laugh. "Go on in. She is already asking for you and her brother. I don't mind telling you, if she keeps up like this, it will be one for the record books."

"Thank you!" I hugged him, and Bruce shook his hand as the automatic doors granted us entry into ICU.

As soon as we entered Ruby's room, she greeted us with a weak smile.

"Cy! What are you doin' here so early? You hate mornings! Hi Bruce. Ain't you supposed to be at work?"

"Ruby, you did great. You sure gave us a scare, though." I weaved my way through the tubes to kiss her on the forehead.

"That's what they told me. I need to get my car. I left it at that rest stop."

"The first thing we are doing is calling your brother."

She seemed surprised that he knew. "You didn't worry him about me, did you?"

"I did worry him a great deal. We thought we were going to lose you, Ruby!"

I called the prison and was pleased to hear the voice of the sergeant who had helped us last night. I knew he'd been praying for Ruby. When I told him that Ruby was alive and doing well, I could hear genuine relief in his voice.

"Oh man, I am so happy for them. I'll go find him and get him in here to talk to her, if she's able to talk."

"She is sitting up ready and waiting."

"What's your cell number again? I'm going to have to call you collect. I'm sorry about that." He apologized for the prison rules.

"Not a problem, we'll wait to hear from you."

About ten minutes later my phone rang, and I handed it directly to Ruby to answer.

We left the room and gave them some privacy. When we

returned to her room, she had a trail of tears spilling down her face.

"He was so happy. I ain't never heard him cry and laugh so much at the same time," she reported while wiping her eyes and face with a tissue. "Sounded like he was scared outta his mind. Thought I was dead!"

Ruby didn't seem to understand how seriously ill she had been.

"God just keeps saving you for something special he has planned for you, Ruby," Bruce told her.

"Well, I ain't got no idea what he's got in mind for this old bird, but I'll do my best," she replied as her eyes fluttered closed. In a moment she was fast asleep.

We left to let her rest. The twenty-four hours the doctors needed in order to see if she was going to make it were almost up, but we went off the clock knowing God had pushed up the time line, and she was going to live.

TWENTY-SIX

A Clean Start

<hr>

*W*hitney and I decided it would be nice for Ruby to come home to a clean apartment after being in the hospital, so we went to her place to do a little spiffing up. We also wanted to feed the cats and bring Layla to our house.

Ruby must have been feeling very sick for a while because her apartment was a total disaster.

There were dirty dishes piled on the counters and in the sink. The cat box was overflowing, along with the ashtrays. Her papers and eclectic assortment of stuff were scattered everywhere. Laundry was heaped on the chairs and couches, evidently doubling as beds for the cats.

This really wasn't like Ruby. While she had never been very concerned about clutter, she always kept her place as clean as possible.

She had been keeping to herself a lot lately and making trips to the doctor. She kept telling me she had the flu and the doctor said to just rest and drink liquids. When I'd drop by with groceries, she'd open the door as far as the chain lock would allow and insist that I leave the groceries outside her door because she didn't want me to get sick. Each time I caught a glimpse of her, she was wearing her long flannel nightgown.

Now seeing the state of things, I felt I had not been a very good friend in recent weeks. I had been trying to keep to our new boundaries, and now I regretted it.

And what in the world was she doing driving down to see her brother if she was this sick? No wonder she collapsed at the rest stop.

Whitney and I surveyed the job ahead of us and knew we were out-trashed and outmatched. Ruby would be home in a couple of days, though, so we gave it our best effort. We went to the store to pick up every kind of cleaning supply we could think of as well as fresh kitty litter, cat food, dog food, and all of Ruby's favorite foods. Well, that's not true, we stuck with her favorite foods that were good for her since her *favorite* foods were all chocolate covered.

We called a friend who had a brother in the carpet cleaning business, and before long he arrived to shampoo the carpets and furniture. We laundered clothes, washed dishes, and wiped all the surfaces with our extensive supply of products.

We found her scrapbook of postcards. There were over fifty postcards chronicling our family's travels. Many of the pages appeared to have been turned often. She told us she loved to imagine being in all those places.

Three days later, Layla accompanied me to pick Ruby up from the hospital and bring her home to her nice clean apartment. A home health nurse came later in the day, and we set up Ruby's very complicated medication regime. Thankfully, Medicaid would provide physical and occupational therapists, who would visit Ruby daily for several weeks. She needed wound care, therapy, and rest.

Her recovery was steady and miraculous.

Our son, Ryan, helped me pick her car up from the Jelly Stone Park rest stop. I am not kidding, there is even a huge Yogi Bear cutout not too far from where her car was safely parked. We went in to tell Shirley, the ranger, that Ruby was alive and well.

"Praise Jesus!" she exclaimed. "I been watchin' over her car and praying she'd be alright. I thought she was going to die on the way to the hospital. I've never seen anyone so pale." She went on to relive the whole experience in great detail.

I followed Ryan in my car as he drove Ruby's car back to her apartment. He parked it where she could see it from her patio window.

Ruby, Layla, her cats, and her car were all back home and settled in.

Ruby was lying in bed as I readied to leave.

"I'm going to have a clean start, Cy," she announced. "I ain't gonna smoke no more."

"Ruby!" I clapped my hands and went back to give her another hug. "I am so proud you!" As I was hugging her, I lifted the pack of cigarettes from her nightstand. I asked, "May I?"

"What? You ain't gonna start smokin' now, are you?" Ruby's grin told me she knew better.

"I might have to take it up, if you keep scaring me to death." I teased. "No, these are going in the trash."

"No, don't trash 'em. Give 'em to one of them poor fellows on the street corners beggin' for food. I'm sure they could use a smoke." She was serious.

Oh, Ruby, Ruby, Ruby.

TWENTY-SEVEN

God Only Knows

After her surgery, Ruby discovered that trips to visit her brother in prison became nearly impossible. The combination of abdominal discomfort and the traumatic memory of her last trip made the three-hour drive very difficult.

One day Sam called Ruby and told her the other inmates had convinced him that, if he kept insisting he was innocent, he would never be paroled. Their advice? Confess to the crime, even though he had no memory of committing it.

After Ruby's near-death experience Sam became more wretched and broken over his inability to help his beloved sister. He told Ruby he was going to confess at his next hearing. He tried to convince her it was the only way he was ever going to be able to get out and take care of her.

Ruby was inconsolable. She called me, panic-stricken.

"Cy, my brother says he is going to confess to the crime he didn't commit after almost thirty years of sayin' he didn't do it!"

This wasn't the first time Sam had considered this tactic. I'd written him a letter talking him out of a similar plan several years ago. Ruby remembered the letter now.

"Cy, remember the letter you wrote him before? I got me the copy you gave me right here. "He needs to read it again. I know he wants out for me, but I don't want him out if it means he has to lie and say he done a horrible crime. I know my brother. He ain't the one who done it!"

"Ruby, let's go visit him this Friday and talk with him; bring the letter." I suggested, hoping that seeing him would make her feel better.

"When I go see him I am down for days. It is so hard on me, but I know how lonely he is. Okay, I'll try." She sounded less enthusiastic than I expected. "He's been feelin' so low. I gotta talk him out sayin' he done somethin' he ain't done."

A few days later we made the trip.

Following the prison entry protocol, Ruby and I waited for her brother to come into the visitors' area. He joined us at a table we had chosen as far from the other visitors and their families as possible. The sight of the kids and their mothers visiting their husbands and dads was always so unsettling for me. I struggled to hold back the tears.

Ruby's brother looked very thin and much older than the last time I'd seen him. He embodied hopelessness.

"Thank you for coming and bringing Ruby today, Cy," he said, his eyes filling with tears. "I'm so happy to see you alive, Sis. I never been more scared in my life than when Cy called me from that hospital. I ain't never prayed so hard." He reached for her hand.

"I'm sorry you had to worry like that. Wish you ain't even been told about it until it was over."

"She's pretty tough. I'm tellin' you," I chimed in. "The doctors are amazed by her recovery. It's a God thing!"

Sam nodded. "God sure did perform a miracle for you, Sis. I hope you thank the Good Man upstairs every night like I do."

Ruby shrugged. "I don't know why God wants to keep an old bird like me on this earth when there's plenty of people that deserve to be here more, but I'm thankful to Him."

"Ruby," I chided lightly, "I would be very sad if I had one less 'old bird' to hang out with. And I'd appreciate fewer disparaging age remarks since I am just five years younger than you!" I tried to lighten the mood. "I've got some tokens for the vending machines, who wants a snack?"

"I like them Snickers Bars," Sam admitted. "I like Coke too."

"Ruby?"

"You gonna let me have a Hershey Bar and a cup of coffee?"

"Promise no more chocolate this week, and you'll eat only half of it?" I asked in a mothering tone.

"I ain't promisin' nothin'." Ruby was not in the mood for my negotiating, and I understood this was not the time to push her.

I volunteered to wander off to another table and let them spend some time visiting on their own, but they insisted I stay with them. I don't remember what we talked about. Probably my family and Ruby's recovery. Her brother tried not to complain much in front of Ruby, but the food situation always came up. Never having had prison food, I didn't really have much to add. Bruce could probably relate better since my cooking probably bears some resemblance.

I wondered if Ruby was going to give him the letter I had written a few years ago or bring up her distress over the idea of him confessing at his pending hearing. It had been one of the reasons for coming. But she never brought it up.

Ruby grew tired quickly and, after an hour or so, we said our goodbyes, and the guard took Sam back to his cell. Guards escorted Ruby and me to the shuttle area, so we could catch the next bus back to the car lot.

Ruby was quiet and slept most of the way back to her apartment. We stopped once for a drive-through hamburger and drink. She ate about half of it and wrapped the rest up for later. In true Ruby form, she ordered extra ketchup, mayo, and mustard packets for her stockpile.

When I dropped her off, I walked her to her door and asked if I could come in for a minute. She said she was pretty tired but, agreed, for a minute.

I had a quick look around and checked her refrigerator. "Do you need anything?" I asked as I was casually opening the refrigerator.

"Nah, I got all I need."

The refrigerator seemed fairly well stocked, and stacks of Mighty Dog and Fancy Feast cans revealed that her animals were covered for the current calendar year. My eyes landed on the ashtray on her kitchen table with a few cigarette butts. It seemed like a day to keep my judgmental remarks to myself.

"I was just thinking, Ruby, if you ever get sick again or your nurse needs to call me, I think I'll write my name and phone number on a piece of paper and tape it on the inside of your front door." I started looking for the tape, pen, and paper.

"That's a good idea." She agreed.

"Also, I kind of thought you were going to bring the letter you wanted your brother to read again today. The one I wrote him five years ago about confessing. Did you change your mind?" I asked gently.

"Nah, I mailed it to him yesterday. I wasn't sure if the guard would let me hand him a paper or if they'd take it from him. It was my only copy. Do you have a copy?"

I did, and I promised to make her a copy to replace the one she had mailed.

As I pulled away from Ruby's apartment and began the drive back to my house, I thought about the letter I had penned to Sam five years ago. The words in my letter expressed my deepest longing for Sam, and for Ruby too. I wanted more than anything for both of them to thrive in a personal relationship with Jesus.

This is what I wrote to Sam:

Good morning,

I just finished speaking with Ruby and she was very worried about the letter you sent to her. The reason I am writing is because as you know, I am a Christian and my faith is my life. It is my trust in the Lord that led me to Ruby in the first place. God loves Ruby very much (as He does you). He knew Ruby needed a friend, and He honored me by trusting me to be that friend to your sister.

I try to explain God's love to Ruby, and truthfully it is hard to explain why some people endure more suffering in their lives than others. But I do know that God loves each of us so very much he allowed His perfect Son to die a terrible, painful, humiliating death on the Cross to pay for our sins. ALL of us have sinned in our lives. God knew the day that He made us that we would. But He wanted to "pay" our way back home to Him through his Son, Jesus Christ. Nothing we can do through good works or giving or helping others or any amount of wealth or status will earn us a spot in Heaven. It has already been earned by Christ for us with His death on the Cross. It is only by confessing our sins to Jesus Christ and believing He is the Son of God, who was nailed to a tree for us and asking Christ into our hearts that we can have faith in our eternity in Heaven.

Ruby is very strong in her sense of right and wrong, truth and lies. She is a remarkable woman who loves you and grieves over the life you are enduring in prison, but she believes regardless of the consequences here on earth, that you must be truthful. God only knows the truth about whether you are guilty of the crime for which you have spent so many years in prison. She knows you worry about her, her health and well-being, but she wants you to know she does not want you to confess to something you have maintained your innocence of for so long, on the "chance" it will help you be released.

No one who has not been in prison can pretend to imagine what it must be like for you every day. Ruby doesn't know, I don't know. But she believes with all of her heart that if you didn't commit the crime, you should never say that you did. I can't tell you how much I hesitate to offer any advice other than the words of my heart which are those I've just written.

My faith has seen me through many difficult times. Many Christians question God's existence and reasoning at some time in their lives. As I read the Bible and study God's Word, I realize that there is and always will be injustice in this world, but it is Christ who will judge us in our final breath, and no one comes to the Father, except through the Son.

I pray for Ruby and for you daily. I ask for God's wisdom. I wish I had the perfect thing to say to ease both of your suffering. All I know is God has a plan for each of us; He never said we wouldn't suffer in this life, but He did promise He would be with us and get us through it—we just need to ask and believe. I pray you will ask Christ into your heart, seek His advice and ask Him to "hold your hand." That's what my grandmother and mother always told me to do and when I do, there is sincerely a sense of peace that follows.

Holding you in prayer,

Cy

TWENTY-EIGHT

It's Just Lunch

---

*B*y Thanksgiving, Ruby seemed to have her appetite back. She was looking forward to the croissants, dressing and, of course, the gravy.

"Do you have them cranberries I like?" she asked as soon as she arrived at our house.

Ah yes, and the cranberries.

That year, when we went around the table sharing what we were thankful for, pretty much everyone said "Ruby!" After all, it had been less than two months since we'd almost lost her.

Christmas on Ruby Trust Court was a full house. We had family visiting from out of town and from around town too. Ruby came midafternoon wearing her red Santa Cat Sweater and reindeer earrings, and driving her newer, smaller redder car we'd purchased to replace the Taurus wagon that had given up on being a car several months prior.

Ruby was always a bit overwhelmed just after dinner and was ready to leave. As expected, the promise of dessert detained her a bit longer; there was no way she would leave before pie and ice cream. After dessert, we packed up her goody bag and waved her off before it got too late. She always called to let us know she arrived home safely.

Another year of crying, laughing, celebrating, and . . . phew, we made it through.

In April 2010, Ruby and I celebrated a decade of friendship.

It made me think of the dating company It's Just Lunch! Of course, the angle is that there's no pressure of an evening date and if things don't go well at lunch, that's it! It's over!

Although Ruby and I began our relationship thinking "it was just lunch," we were both grateful for the many lunches we had shared.

And now, ten years later, we were sitting at Ruby's favorite Mexican restaurant, remembering highlights (and some lowlights) of our ten years together as friends. Over chips and salsa, we took a trip down memory lane. We started by remembering, in no particular order, all the people who had reached out to help Ruby. There was our family optometrist, Dr. Knapp, who donated eye exams and glasses for Ruby. (He helped her finally get rid of her gigantic duct-taped frames.) We talked about our neighbors, the Barczyks, who gave Ruby gift cards. The many doctors and nurses who gave her an extra dose of care and compassion when she was in their care. My friends Sue and Martha, who were on call when I was out of town. We remembered how Martha had cheered Ruby on, risking her very life to help Ruby get her driver's license. There was the manager of Ruby's first apartment building who gave her a couch. My nephew, Kevin, and brother-in-law, Dale, who helped Ruby when she needed to pick up furniture or move. There was the lady at the housing department who helped Ruby with her Section 8 and got her into an apartment in record time. We talked about the surgeons who had recently saved her life, the chaplains who had provided such comfort, and the sergeant at

Sam's prison who had prayed for both Ruby and Sam. We were also thankful for my Bible study members, the Girlz, and many other friends and family who had prayed Ruby through surgeries and illnesses.

"Whitney and Bruce," Ruby added to our list. "They done so much for me. I can never repay them. You got yourself a real fine man in that Bruce. Whitney is very special to me. I don't know your son that well, but he is always very nice to me whenever I seen him."

"Remember when you wouldn't even get in the car with me?" I chided.

"I didn't understand you."

"Understand me?"

"It didn't make no sense. Why would you want to help me? I didn't trust you." She confessed. "And I couldn't figure out why you trusted me."

"You know why," I said. "I trusted God, and He trusted you."

She poured another half bottle of hot sauce on her enchilada and took a bite. Just looking at it set my hair on fire. She seemed unaffected.

"Ruby," I said, "do you trust me now?"

"With my life."

TWENTY-NINE

October 30, 2010

ello. Am I speaking with Cy DeBoer?"

"Yes." I used my abrupt "this better not be a salesman" voice.

"This is officer Gallegos. with Arapahoe County Sheriff's department. Are you driving?"

"Is this Bruce?"

I was suspicious because sometimes when my husband sees it's me calling him, he loves to answer the phone "Arapahoe County Sheriff's Department" to be funny. (I'm so over it.)

"No. Ma'am," he said calmly. "Again, my name is Officer Gallegos and if you are driving, I would like you to pull your car over to a place where you can safely speak with me."

"Okay, I can pull over just around the corner." I was shaking. I couldn't begin to imagine what was going on. "Okay, I'm parked.

"Alright good. I am sorry to alarm you, but I am calling about your friend, Ruby. I was just at her apartment and saw your name and number taped to her door asking to be called in the event of an emergency."

"Yes? Is she alright? Where is she?" I could barely breathe.

"She called 911 about an hour ago. When I arrived the EMTs were working over her on the floor of her living room. They took her to Swedish Hospital. Do you know where that is?"

"Yes, I am about fifteen minutes away."

"Miss DeBoer, please don't speed, drive slowly and carefully. I don't think you need to rush." Then he added gently, "When the ambulance left, they didn't have their sirens on."

"Are you saying Ruby is dead already?" I was choking on my tears.

"That is what I presume based on the lack of sirens and the demeanor of the emergency team. I would also caution you not to go to her place by yourself. Due to the efforts to revive her, things are in pretty bad shape near the entrance and the bedroom. I am very sorry."

He asked if I had a pen and paper to write his number down and to call him if I needed anything or had any questions.

As I wrote down his number he added, "Do you have anyone to call to be with you at the hospital?"

"Yes, my daughter and my husband."

"Okay, do you know if she has any other relatives who need to be notified?"

"Just me."

"Are you going to be alright?" he asked one more time before saying goodbye.

"I'm alright. Thank you for being so kind. I truly appreciate your sincere concern. God bless you."

"God bless you; I'll pray for you. Goodbye."

I called Whitney on my way to the hospital. She answered

the phone and when I told her the sad news, she said she would meet me at the hospital. I left Bruce a message on his cell. He was enjoying the last of golf season and probably wouldn't get it for a little while.

In truth, I don't really remember arriving at the hospital. I must have parked somewhere, but I only recall running into the emergency entrance, giving Ruby's name, and asking to see her. I felt she was still alive, that there was a mistake. Maybe we could have a few minutes together; I could hold her hand; we could pray.

They must have been busy because the person at the desk just pointed to the doors over her shoulder while she remained on the phone.

I walked through the doors and started wandering down the hall looking for Ruby. The first few rooms were either empty or the curtains were drawn, and none of the voices I heard were Ruby's. As I came to an open door with no curtain, I saw a little body covered head to toe with a sheet, and I felt a hand touch me on the back of my shoulder.

"Are you here for Ruby Jean? I am sorry no one spoke to you before you came back here. I don't know if you want to go in and see her." The nurse just stood there in the hall with me as I stared at the outline of my friend under a thin sheet.

"Was she dead when she arrived?" I asked, wondering if I'd been here just a few minutes earlier, I might have been able to say goodbye.

"It's my understanding she passed away in the ambulance."

I slid down against the wall to the floor with my head in my hands and started sobbing and shaking. I rocked from side to side, "Ruby, Ruby, Ruby," I repeated over and over. The nurse eased me to my feet and took me to a private waiting room.

"The attending physician will be in to talk to you soon, and I've paged our chaplain to come visit with you as well." She pointed me toward a comfortable chair in the small room and started to leave.

When Whitney came into the room, she had tears in her eyes. "I'm so sorry, Mom." She hugged me tightly.

"Thanks for coming, honey. I am in shock. Not sure why. She was in such poor health from the day we met her.

"Just think if you hadn't met her, she wouldn't have lived anywhere near this long," Whitney pointed out, hoping to console me.

We were telling Ruby stories when the chaplain came in and caught us laughing through our tears. Both Whitney and I had dozens of tissues wadded in our hands and in our laps. He was kind and prayed with us. The doctor came in while we were praying. He stood and listened as we told the chaplain about Ruby, how she came into our lives and had changed us for the better.

"You are not related to Ruby, then?" the doctor gently inquired.

"No, but other than her brother in prison, we are the only family she has."

"I am so sorry but I'm going to have to ask you some questions," he said, sitting beside me and speaking quietly and gently.

I didn't mind telling him about Ruby. I never minded telling anyone. Ruby's story always made people more thoughtful and a better version of themselves. Ruby did that to people.

After we talked for several minutes he asked, "Do you have power of attorney and does she have a will?"

"Yes, I am and yes she does."

"Do you know if she had made any plans for death? A funeral plan, a cemetery plot?" he continued.

"No, she struggled to live. She didn't have the means to prepare to die. Do you know of a mortuary where we can send her remains? I do know she wanted to be cremated."

"We have a list; you can make some calls while you are here. We would like to know as soon as possible so we can make arrangements to have her transferred."

"Thank you. I will take care of it right away."

"Take your time here. Just relax and make the calls. I do want to tell you how touched I am by your story. You obviously loved her very much." He looked at Whitney and added, "I can tell she was also very important to you. Thank you for what you did for Ruby." He shook our hands and started toward the door. "There will be no autopsy; she died from natural causes—heart failure."

The chaplain stepped forward to assume his duties once the doctor left. He went to get the list of mortuaries. We selected one and made the call. I spoke with the administrator, and we agreed to meet on Monday to go over the details.

Bruce called and was heartbroken for me, for Sam, and for our family. I called Ryan and filled him in on our sad news. Although he didn't know Ruby as well since he didn't live in Colorado during most of our time with her, he knew the impact she had made on all of us. He cared for her.

We went home that night with aching hearts. We told more Ruby stories. We thought a lot about the wonder of God. We talked about how he had chosen to put us in Ruby's life and Ruby in ours.

We talked about the what ifs. What if I hadn't been

"shoved" that April day over a decade ago? We would never know the answer for sure. But one thing we *did* know, a Ruby —far more precious than diamonds—had been given to our care for a season.

We were so humbled by God's and Ruby's Trust.

THIRTY

Because I Knew You

The call to Sam on the day of Ruby's death was one of the most difficult calls I had ever made. I was able to arrange for the chaplain to be with him when I gave him the terrible news. He immediately asked if we could talk to "somebody" and make arrangements for him to attend her memorial service.

DESPITE OUR FERVENT PLEAS, the Colorado Corrections Department would not let her brother attend Ruby's memorial service and deliver his eulogy. He sent it to us to read on his behalf.

Bruce read Sam's eulogy at Ruby's memorial service a month after her passing:

November 29, 2010

I am like a lion that has lost a loved one... Part of his

family. My heart roars full of pain like a lost lion… But then, I hear a soft voice whisper in my ear, "It is okay, my brother, I am still with you." My heart, my very soul cries out with so much pain, tears run like rain down my face. I remember the precious times when my dear sister Ruby would pull the old, little red wagon down the ole' dusty dirt road. She would be laughing, I would be crying… Her face would glow that gentle smile, and she would say, "Don't cry little brother I ain't gonna let nothing happen to you." Every day of my life I remembered those comforting days and how the whisper of her voice would reassure my place in this world.

She showed her unfailing patience when I climbed behind the wheel of the Mercury and she taught me how to drive the manual transmission, laughing as we went down that same ole dirt road.

We always knew this day might come. Yet, she always reminded me of the strength that was part of life at a time of worry and uncertainty. Still, I felt weak and she always told me to be assured in the strength of love and God.

Ruby was the kindest and strongest woman I ever knew. "Carry on little brother, carry on," she would always say. She always called me little brother when she reminded me that she will always be with me. Though she is gone in body her spirit lives on. Her strength and kindness she left in my heart. To all that knew her she will remain an example of the way we all should live. I have in me her determination, her smile and her faith. I hurt, I am empty, I am sad, and I understand because of her wisdom and the faith in God she instilled in me. God had other plans, other duties for her to perform. I will miss her and will likely never find a day empty of a thought of her.

Ruby, I love you and miss you. Know this—I will continue on and make your love for me live on. Someday we will again walk that ole dusty road.

Love,

Your Little Brother, XO

BRUCE READ the letter with tears in his eyes, pausing more than once to try to compose himself. I think he was not prepared for how deeply Ruby and her brother had entrenched themselves in his heart.

We sent notices of Ruby's passing and information about her memorial to our close friends, my Bible study friends, a few of Ruby's friends from her first apartment community, and members of Bruce's and my families.

Over forty people were gathered on November 28, 2011, in the Fireside Room of Cherry Hills Community Church. Ruby would have been astounded to see all the people who had cared about her and prayed for her over the nearly eleven years she'd been in our lives. They sat reverently at round tables set for lunch in the cozy, unpretentious room.

A long banquet table to the side of the room displayed memorabilia from her apartment, mostly her brother's art and her leather handbag. I saved a box of all the beautiful handmade cards her brother had sent to our family over the years. It was placed next to Ruby's book of postcards from our family trips alongside our family Christmas cards in frames she'd carefully chosen at Arch. These few items seemed a meager representation of a life spanning sixty-four years, but they were a huge testimony to her love for her brother and for our family. When

Ruby loved, it was with all her heart. We will always feel extraordinarily honored that, along with Sam, we were considered Ruby's most beloved.

Our pastor and friend of many years, Brett Garretson, gave a beautiful message to honor Ruby. Even though he didn't know her personally, he knew of her and memorialized her with grace and care. During his message, he admitted that when he first heard the story of Ruby, he questioned if it could possibly be true. "This is a God story" he proclaimed. "The DeBoer's story is God's story. It is a story of God's promises and provisions that are granted when we step out in faith."

He spoke of the harsh reality of Ruby's life—her captivity, health, finances, distrust—that made her world small and protective. If only she knew to rely on the Lord's promise: " I will never leave you, I will never forsake you."

When Brett introduced me to speak, I did my best to follow the twenty-page script I had labored over for days. I lost my place in under two minutes. Fighting back tears that blurred my vision, I wandered rather incoherently through Ruby's and my story. Fortunately everyone there knew most of it.

Next Whitney came up to share her thoughts. She had met Ruby the same day I did. Whitney had been thirteen then. Now, an eloquent twenty-three-year-old woman who loves the Lord, Whitney recited the "Footprints" poem that meant so much to both Whitney and Ruby. In fact, Whitney had given Ruby a framed copy, which she'd hung on her bedroom wall. The vivid picture of the single set of footprints in the sand, which represented the most difficult times in our lives when Jesus carried us, was embedded in our minds as Whitney continued. "All of you in this room have been part of my family's 'walk in the sand,' and all of you in some way have been a part of Ruby's path. If not directly, certainly through your prayers. Prayers leave footprints."

Then she added, "I guess one of the most important things I want you to understand, besides the peace and comfort that comes with knowing our Ruby is in heaven now with no pain or suffering or sadness, is that this story doesn't have to be rare. It is so easy to become footprints in the lives of those around us. Being selfless in helping someone when they need it most—when there is nothing in it for you—is such a beautiful thing. You never know where or when a Ruby will cross your road. You just need to have an open heart to hear God speak and be willing to listen. My mom listened. We can all listen."

The room was still.

Our friend and beautiful vocalist from our church sang "For Good," which I requested because it perfectly expressed what I wanted Ruby to hear from me. There is a line in the song that says; "Because I knew you, I've been changed for the better—I have been changed for good." That is what Ruby did for me. She changed me for the better, and she changed me for good.

Pastor Garretson ended with these words: "Thank you to all for coming here today to honor Ruby. Whitney purchased one hundred pairs of mittens and gloves so as you leave, please take a couple pairs of them to share with someone in need of warmth in honor of Ruby. Also take one of the shiny red ornaments to hang on your tree this Christmas as a visual reminder of our friend, Ruby.

He closed in prayer, then led us in singing Amazing Grace:
"Through many dangers, toils and snares,
I have already come;
'Tis Grace that brought me safe thus far
And Grace will lead me Home"

· · ·

AT THE END of the long banquet table on a stand was a small red chest that held Ruby's ashes. I said to Ruby, "I have your ashes, my precious friend. Thank you for your trust in life and in death, you changed me forever. You are home, Ruby."

Epilogue

*S*even months after Ruby's death, Bruce and I were called to a meeting with a panel from the Department of Corrections and Arapahoe County. We walked into a county building room not knowing what to expect other than it was about Ruby's brother. After several panel members asked Bruce and I about our relationship to her brother, referring to all the letters and hearings, Bruce was asked to speak.

He gave an eloquent speech declaring, "Regardless of why Sam was in prison for thirty-two years, if the system ever honored rehabilitation, this man deserves a second chance. He is not the same man who entered prison over three decades ago." He added, "Cy and I will be here to support him in any way we can. We want to see him spend the remainder of his life using the skills he has learned to become a productive member of society. Please give him that opportunity."

Two weeks later, seven months following Ruby's death, Sam called to tell us that a majority of the panel had voted to allow him to be released to a halfway house in Arapahoe County. He was not actually on parole—at least not yet. He would still be under the control of Colorado Department of Corrections, and the slightest misstep on his part would land him back in prison.

Another book could be written about the uphill battle Sam faced at every turn. No job, no computer skills, no money, and poor health, barely scratches the surface of his encumbrances. Bruce and I continue to be amazed by his tenacity and courage to beat the odds and to keep on keeping on.

A prison ministry leader at our church, Skipp Starr of Refuge City Ministries, introduced us to a wonderful woman, Marcia Hannah, who advocates for prisoners through her ministry A Future and a Hope. Marcia came alongside Sam and helped him find housing. Our friend Gary Roberts, one of the contractors who built our house on Ruby Trust Court and an amazing ambassador for Christ, gave Ruby's brother jobs whenever he could.

I'd told Ruby we would watch over Sam in prison. I also promised her that we would watch over him if he were ever released—a vow I never through we would get the chance to fulfill.

His first six years out of prison—but still under the jurisdiction of the Colorado Department of Corrections—were so difficult. Most men who are incarcerated for thirty-two years have a difficult time surviving the rigors of reentry into the world. Sam had so many boundaries: an ankle monitor, curfews, and constant rejection by employers where he sought to work. He was a skilled plumber and electrician, but he was also an ex-convict, which trumped all else.

Still, he persevered without bitterness or anger. He just wanted to work. He wanted to begin a new life. He prayed daily. We gave him the devotional book *Jesus Calling*, and no one could have been more devoted to it than him.

One day he visited Tom, a friend he had met in prison who had been released and was in a medical rehabilitation nursing center. While there, Sam met a new friend of Tom's, a woman rehabilitating from a very painful and damaged back. Every time Sam visited Tom, he visited with Christine. Soon they'd become very close.

Bruce and I didn't even know about her until Sam asked us to meet her one day. We took them to a casual dinner.

They were obviously in love.

———

In August 2017, Sam and Christine were married in our backyard. Being blessed with the most amazing friends, a week before the wedding, my friend Nettie—who never met the bride before but wanted her to feel like a bride—had a beautiful luncheon bridal shower with five of my close friends in attendance. The couple registered at Target and, between the shower and wedding guests, their requests were all filled. Even more amazing, the gifts were given by people who had yet to meet the happy couple.

Judy Weaver, my best friend who has shared everything in my life since we met at age thirteen, arrived the night before the wedding and blew up balloons, set the tables, decorated, and made a playlist of the bride's favorite songs for the wedding.

On the actual day of the wedding, our friends and family joined in the celebration and brought beautiful gifts and well wishes. Dutch Franz, a dear friend and pastor, performed the tender ceremony in front of the waterfall in our yard. We placed a photograph of Ruby on a large rock near where the other guests were seated. She watched over the ceremony with love.

Bruce and I were the best man and matron of honor.

Six months after his wedding, Ruby's brother, thirty-eight years after being incarcerated, was paroled on Valentine's Day 2018.

One of our Ruby Tuesday lunches

Grandma and Ruby chatting

"Ruby's" Street Sign

Ruby passes her drivers test

The Wedding Party: Sam, Christine, Bruce and Cy

Ruby watches her brother's wedding

About the Author

Cy DeBoer is a published author, columnist, and inspirational speaker. She is the founder of Bin Blessed (www.binblessed.com), a charity that provides assistance to There With Care, an organization that provides support to families with a child in medical crisis.

Cy and her husband, Bruce, have two adult children, and two grandchildren. They live in Castle Rock, Colorado.

Follow Cy on her website: cydeboer.com